100
YEARS OF BRITISH MUSIC

A photographic tribute to some of the greatest
songwriters and composers of all time.

100
YEARS OF
BRITISH
MUSIC

A photographic tribute to some of the greatest
songwriters and composers of all time.

OMNIBUS PRESS

LONDON / NEW YORK / PARIS / SYDNEY / COPENHAGEN / BERLIN / MADRID / TOKYO

Copyright © 2014 PRS for Music.

Published by Omnibus Press (a division of Music Sales Limited).

Concept by Guy Fletcher OBE.

New photography by Lucy Sewill.
Archive photography research by Jacqui Black.
Text by Christopher Welch.

Designed by Paul Tippett and Adrian Andrews for Vitamin P.

Project Managers: Rosie Blanchard (PRS for Music) and Tom Farncombe (Music Sales Limited).

Writer and composer relations: Myles Keller
Photo and copy coordination: Eileen Fitches

With thanks to: Chris Butler, Ray Luker, Linda Groundsell, Paul Sims, Eddie Gregson, Estelle Morris, John Minch, Paulette Long, Lynsey de Paul and Vanessa Reed.

ISBN 978-1-78305-507-4
Order Number: OP55759

Exclusive Distributors
Music Sales Limited
14/15 Berners Street, London W1T 3LJ
United Kingdom.

Music Sales Corporation
257 Park Avenue South, New York NY 10010
United States of America.

Macmillan Distribution Services
56 Parkwest Drive, Derrimut, Vic 3030
Australia.

Printed in China.

A catalogue record for this book is available from the British Library.

www.prsformusic.com
www.omnibuspress.com

Honours
KBE: Knight Commander of the Most Excellent Order of the British Empire
CBE: Commander of the Most Excellent Order of the British Empire
OBE: Officer of the Most Excellent Order of the British Empire
MBE: Member of the Most Excellent Order of the British Empire
OM: Order of Merit
CH: Order of the Companions of Honour
LVO: Lieutenant of the Royal Victorian Order

CLARENCE HOUSE

This splendid centenary book offers an historical snapshot of British creators, whose extraordinary talents have shaped our music culture over the last century.

From classical composers such as Benjamin Britten and Sir Edward Elgar to contemporary artists like John Lennon, Sir Paul McCartney, David Bowie and Gary Barlow – our country has been blessed with exceptional music talent which, through the past one hundred years, has been nurtured, supported and promoted by PRS for Music. This global impact is worthy of special celebration, which is why I am so delighted to be able to contribute to this book and to offer my warmest congratulations to PRS for Music.

May this country enjoy another one hundred years of fine musical success and in the meantime, I do hope you enjoy this visual journey through times gone by.

CONTENTS

INTRODUCTION

U K legislation to license the public use of music has been in place since 1842. The law was designed to provide some recompense for authors and composers whose music and songs were being performed in theatres, cafes and music halls. Predictably there was strong resistance to this from promoters and even music publishers, resulting in little or no money flowing to creators for many years. In 1875 an opportunist named Harry Wall opened a business in Islington which he called 'The Copyright and Performing Right Protection Office'. He set about selling performance licences to anyone who could be persuaded to buy. However, his nefarious manner of trading brought him before a judge who sentenced him to three months imprisonment for contravention of the Solicitors' Act: an inauspicious start to our noble cause.

The 1911 Copyright Act strengthened the law and UK publishers and writers, inspired by the success of the French performing right society SACEM (which had been collecting royalties since 1850), agreed to form the society we have today. Initial meetings were held in 1913, chaired by William Boosey, and a committee of eight writers and eight publishers was assembled (see picture on page 12). Initial funding was obtained by gathering £50 from each publisher and the Performing Right Society opened for business on March 6, 1914.

Over the ensuing 100 years, PRS has successfully administered the Performing Right for almost all British writers and publishers. From those early days when music was primarily disseminated by sheet music sales and live theatre performance, through the development of the record industry, the advent of broadcasting in 1922 and television in 1934, right up to date with music being available globally on the internet. The society's structure and objectives have changed very little. Still a membership organisation owned by its 100,000+ members, PRS has established a peerless worldwide reputation for excellence in licensing, collection and distribution of performance royalties.

Of course, PRS has only been able to do this because it represents some of the finest composers, songwriters and music publishers in the world and manages a phenomenal repertoire of their music of all genres. The purpose of this book is to celebrate our centenary and bring you a collection of photographs of some of these wonderful individuals who have contributed so much to our global music culture.

Guy Fletcher OBE
Chairman, PRS

THE PERFORMING RIGHT SOCIETY LTD FOUNDERS, 1914

The 18 members of the first society board united to protect the performing right for British composers and publishers.

Top row:

Worton David

H. S. J. Booth

John Woodhouse

Pierre G. Sarpy

Adrian Ross

B. Feldman

Middle row:

Herman Finck

David Day

William Boosey

Oliver Hawkes

Paul A. Rubens

Bottom row:

Henry E. Pether

Hermann Lohr

Arthur Edward Bosworth

Lionel Monckton

Charles Volkert

Harold Simpson

Bennett Scott

SIR HUBERT PARRY

Sir Charles Hubert Hastings Parry, composer, music teacher and historian, is best known for his choral song 'Jerusalem' and the coronation anthem 'I Was Glad'. Born in Bournemouth (February 27, 1848), he was educated at Eton and Oxford. He worked as an insurance underwriter until 1887, but continued studying music. In 1883 he became a professor of composition and musical history at the Royal College of Music. Parry composed the oratorios *Judith*, *Job* and *King Saul*, and an opera, *Guinevere*. He also wrote five symphonies, quartets and cantatas and his books included the *Evolution Of The Art Of Music* (1896) and a study of Bach (1909). Parry, acclaimed as the finest English composer since Purcell, was considered to be an influence on Edward Elgar. His students at the Royal College included Vaughan Williams and Gustav Holst. After contracting Spanish influenza during the post-World War I pandemic he died aged 70 on October 17, 1918.

FREDERICK WEATHERLY

Frederick Edward Weatherly enjoyed a career as a lawyer, author, lyricist and radio broadcaster. Weatherly's best-known songs are 'Danny Boy' and 'Roses Of Picardy'. Born in Portishead, Somerset (October 4, 1848), he was educated at Hereford Cathedral School. He won a scholarship to Brasenose College, Oxford in 1867 and in 1887 he qualified as a barrister, practising in London. Altering the spelling of his first name to 'Frederic', he became a prolific lyricist. An early work was 'The Holy City' (1892) set to music by Stephen Adams. The haunting words to 'Danny Boy' were written in 1910 and set to the old Irish tune 'Londonderry Air'. 'Roses Of Picardy' (1916) was set to music by Haydn Wood. Weatherly also composed 'When We Are Old And Grey' and 'When You Come Home' among dozens of other titles. He died aged 80 on September 7, 1929 and 'The Londonderry Air' was played at his funeral in Bath Abbey.

SIR EDWARD ELGAR OM

As the composer of the much loved *Enigma Variations* (1899) and many other important works, Elgar's genius was responsible for re-establishing English music's status throughout the world. 'Nimrod' (*Variations*) has won lasting popularity, as has the stirring military march *Pomp And Circumstance No. 1* (1901) from which came 'Land Of Hope And Glory'.

Sir Edward Elgar was born at Broadheath, near Worcester (June 2, 1857), the son of a piano tuner who owned a musical instrument shop. Apart from violin lessons, Elgar was largely self-taught. As a youth he was a church organist and conductor of local bands. After marrying in 1889, he moved to London before settling in Malvern. Success came late. As his fame spread, a three-day Elgar Festival was held in London in 1904 and the composer was knighted and awarded the OM. His first symphony (1908) received over 100 performances in its first year and was followed by major works including Cello Concerto (1919) and *The Dream Of Gerontius* (1900). He became Master of the King's Music in 1924. Sir Edward Elgar died on February 23, 1934.

FREDERICK DELIUS CH

Elgar described Delius as a 'poet and visionary' whose most popular work *On Hearing The First Cuckoo In Spring* (1912) has been hailed as 'exquisite'. An English composer of German descent, Frederick Delius was born in Bradford (January 29, 1862). Despite his obvious musical gifts, his parents planned a commercial career for him. Aged 22 he went to America to manage an orange plantation in Florida but in his leisure time he began studying music. He entered Leipzig Conservatory in 1886 and was befriended by Grieg. From 1888 Delius lived in France, where he composed prolifically in his own individual style, writing six operas including *Koanga* (1895/7) and *A Village Romeo And Juliet* (1899/1901). Smaller orchestral works and larger choral and orchestral pieces *Appalachia*, *Sea Drift* and *A Mass Of Life* (1904/5) followed. Suffering ill health, by 1924 Delius was paralysed and blind. With the help of Eric Fenby, he produced his final works, *A Song Of Summer*, *Idyll* and *Songs Of Farewell*. Delius died aged 72 (June 10, 1934).

SIR EDWARD GERMAN

Famed for his light opera *Merrie England*, the composer Edward
German Jones was adept at blending charming melodies with folk
songs and traditional dances. Born in Whitchurch, Shropshire (February
17, 1862), he played violin and began composing as a youth. He later
studied at the Royal Academy of Music and became a Fellow in 1885.
By 1888 he was musical director at the Globe Theatre, London, providing
incidental music for Shakespearian productions. In 1901 he completed
Arthur Sullivan's comic opera *The Emerald Isle* after the composer's death.
Subsequently he wrote *Merrie England* (1902), which yielded 'The
Yeomen Of England'. This was followed by *Tom Jones* (1907) and *Fallen
Fairies* (1909). He wrote symphonies and orchestral suites but concentrated
on conducting later in life. Knighted in 1928 he was made an Honorary
Freeman of the Worshipful Company of Musicians. As leader of PRS,
he fought for composers' rights to fair compensation. Sir Edward died on
November 11, 1936 aged 74.

SIR HARRY LAUDER

Famed for perennial favourites 'Roamin' In The Gloamin' and 'Keep Right On To The End Of The Road', Lauder was a much loved Scottish comic singer and songwriter. Born Henry Lauder in Portobello, Edinburgh (August 4, 1870), he worked in the coalmines as a young man, where he sang to amuse his workmates. They encouraged him to sing in local halls, which led to him quitting the mines to embark on a career as a professional entertainer billed as Harry Lauder. International fame beckoned when 'I Love A Lassie' was a big hit in 1905. Knighted in 1919 in recognition of his work entertaining the troops during World War I, he regularly toured the United States and Australia clad in his trademark kilt and sporran. Sir Harry appeared in several films and sold over a million records during a 40-year career. He died in Strathaven, Lanarkshire on February 26, 1950.

WILLIAM HENRY SQUIRE

As an instrumentalist, songwriter and early recording artist, William Henry Squire (born August 8, 1871) was a pioneer in many respects. He studied cello at the Royal College of Music and later became the principal cello player with top London orchestras. He popularised the cello as a solo instrument while performing concertos by Elgar and Saint-Saëns in concerts and through his recordings. Squire also wrote his own cello concerto and began writing music for popular songs, collaborating with lyricist Frederick Weatherly. Among his songs were 'A Sergeant Of The Line', 'The Corporal's Ditty', 'In An Old-Fashioned Town' and 'When You Come Home'.

In November 1898 he became one of the first instrumentalists to record his work when he performed 'Simple Aveu' Op. 25 by Francis Thomé in a newly established London studio. He would continue to record for the G&T label, which eventually became HMV, including his own composition 'Serenade' (1911). In 1926 he recorded Saint-Saëns' Cello Concerto No. 1 with the Hallé Orchestra. Squire died in London, aged 91 (March 17, 1963).

RALPH VAUGHAN WILLIAMS OM

A composer of symphonies, operas and chamber music, Vaughan Williams is a towering figure in British classical music. Born in Gloucestershire (October 12, 1872), an early aptitude for composition was encouraged by his parents and later at Charterhouse School. He studied under Charles Stanford at the Royal College of Music, Max Bruch in Berlin and Maurice Ravel in Paris. Despite travels abroad, the English nature of his music was unaffected by European influences. As a result he was hailed as the first important national composer since the 16th century. A first major success was *Sea Symphony* (1910). Later orchestral works included *Fantasia On A Theme By Thomas Tallis* (1909), *A London Symphony* (1914) and *A Pastoral Symphony* (1922). He wrote the ballet *Job* (1930) and the opera *The Pilgrim's Progress* (1948). Also in 1948 he composed music for the film *Scott Of The Antarctic*, on which he later drew in his *Sinfonia Antartica* of 1952. Two more symphonies followed before his death (August 26, 1958), when Vaughan Williams was laid to rest in Westminster Abbey.

GUSTAV HOLST

Holst's *The Planets* was greeted with shock and surprise when it was unveiled in 1914. Nothing like it had been heard before and it was acclaimed as a masterpiece of 20th-century English music. Its seven movements depict the orbiting bodies of the solar system, the varied themes suggesting each planet's character, such as 'Mars, The Bringer Of War' and 'Jupiter, The Bringer Of Jollity'. The latter was partly adapted for the patriotic hymn 'I Vow To Thee, My Country'.

English-born Gustav Theodore Holst (Cheltenham, September 21, 1874) came from a family of professional musicians and hoped to become a pianist. Problems with his right arm meant he had to concentrate on composition while studying at the Royal College of Music. To supplement his income, he took up the trombone as a professional player and became a teacher and musical director at Morley College in 1907. After World War I, *The Planets* was an international success but his reputation was broadly based on a large number of works composed for a wide spectrum of forces – from choral works such as *A Choral Fantasia* (1930) and *Choral Hymns From The Rig Veda* (1908/10), to works for chamber and full orchestra (the *St Paul's Suite* and *Egdon Heath*) and to opera (*The Perfect Fool* and *Savitri*). Holst was acknowledged as an influence on Michael Tippett and Benjamin Britten. He died on May 25, 1934.

ALBERT KETÈLBEY

Ketèlbey's 'In A Monastery Garden' is a delightful, uplifting song that has brought pleasure to millions. Albert Ketèlbey's work was neglected towards the end of his life, yet he was a prolific composer, conductor and pianist who wrote many light music favourites, notably 'In The Moonlight' and 'In A Persian Market'. Born in Birmingham (August 9, 1875) he attended Trinity College of Music and later became a church organist and musical director at London's Vaudeville Theatre where he wrote copious vocal and instrumental pieces. His *Cockney Suite* was much admired by King George V. In 1929 he was proclaimed the UK's 'Greatest Living Composer' by the *Performing Right Gazette*. Ketèlbey died on November 26, 1959, largely forgotten, but in recent years his legacy has gained wider appreciation. In 2003 his 'Bells Across The Meadows' was voted by BBC radio listeners one of the 100 most popular tunes of all time.

PERCY GREENBANK

London-born lyricist Percy Greenbank (January 24, 1878) made an important contribution to some of the most popular musical comedies of the Edwardian era. He collaborated with composers Adrian Ross, Ivan Caryll and Lionel Monckton at the behest of theatre manager George Joseph Edwardes, working on a string of hit shows, notably *The Toreador* (1901), *A Country Girl* (1902), *The Earl And The Girl* (1903) and *The Dancing Mistress* (1912).

Greenbank was the younger brother of successful lyricist Harry Greenbank. He began his career as a journalist writing for *Punch*, *The Sketch* and *The Tatler*. When Harry died, aged just 33, Percy took over his brother's role and wrote copious lyrics for musicals throughout the 1900s. When Edwardes died in 1915, Greenbank carried on writing musical comedies such as *The Boy* (1917). After World War I he mainly worked on adapting theatrical works before enjoying a long retirement. He died aged 90 on December 9, 1968.

JOHN IRELAND

English composer John Nicholson Ireland was born in Bowdon, near Manchester (August 13, 1879) and studied piano, organ and later composition under Charles Stanford at the Royal College of Music, where he later himself became Professor of Composition with E. J. Moeran, Richard Arnell, Geoffrey Bush, Helen Perkin and the young Benjamin Britten among his pupils. Ireland began writing songs and chamber music, and established his reputation with the Violin Sonata No. 1 (1909). His poetic muse was inspired by ancient traditions and places he visited, evident in the piano piece *The Island Spell* (1912) written while staying in Jersey. The writings of Arthur Machen were a lifelong source of inspiration. After two decades in London composing, teaching and serving as organist of St. Luke's, Chelsea, he returned to Guernsey in the Channel Islands just before World War II, but had to be evacuated in 1940 when the Germans invaded. An orchestral work *The Forgotten Rite* (1913) was written in Jersey, while *Mai-Dun* (1921) evoked the large Iron Age hill fort Maiden Castle in Dorset. As well as an immensely popular and much-recorded piano concerto (1930), another work for piano and orchestra (*Legend*, 1933) and a large-scale choral work *These Things Shall Be* (1937, commissioned for the coronation of King George VI), Ireland composed a quantity of chamber music, six volumes of solo piano music, church music, and many songs, notably to texts by Hardy, Masefield ('Sea Fever', 1913) and Housman (the cycle *Land Of Lost Content*, 1921), and a film score, for *The Overlanders* (1946). He retired in 1953 and died aged 82 (June 12, 1962) at his home, Rock Mill – a converted windmill – in Sussex.

KENNETH J. ALFORD

Whistled merrily while accompanied by a strident military brass band, British army soldiers were cheered by the cocksure ditty 'Colonel Bogey'. The march, composed by Kenneth J. Alford, was featured in the 1957 movie *The Bridge On The River Kwai*. The composer was born Frederick Joseph Ricketts in London's East End (February 21, 1881). As a child he was fascinated by street bands and studied piano and organ. He joined the Royal Irish Regiment as a band boy in 1895 and progressed to the Royal Military School of Music. In 1908 he became bandmaster in the 2nd Battalion of the Argyll and Sutherland Highlanders. He wrote their regimental march 'The Thin Red Line' and many more marches under the pen name Kenneth J. Alford, commencing with 'Holyrood' (1911) and followed by 'The Voice Of The Guns' (1917) and 'Dunedin' (1928). His 'Colonel Bogey' theme (1914) was allegedly inspired while playing golf when stationed in Scotland. The popular bandmaster retired from the Royal Marines in 1944 due to ill health and died in Reigate, Surrey (June 1, 1944).

PERCY GRAINGER

Composer and pianist George Percy Grainger, born in Melbourne (July 8, 1882), was encouraged by his mother Rose to study music and art. As a child pianist he was critically acclaimed at home, but left Australia to study in Frankfurt in 1895. Fascinated by Nordic and British music, he moved to London in 1901 where he met Vaughan Williams and Elgar. He also befriended Grieg and Delius. Grainger collected and transcribed folk songs that informed his own work, exemplified by the lively dance themes 'Molly On The Shore', 'Mock Morris' and 'Shepherd's Hey'. 'Country Gardens', one of his most popular compositions, broke all records for sheet music sales. In 1914 he left England for America, where he performed with Nellie Melba. During World War II he toured extensively giving charity concerts, but in the Fifties he suffered ill health and gave up composing. He died in America on February 20, 1961 and his body was flown to Adelaide for burial.

SIR ARNOLD BAX

Arnold Bax achieved success during the Twenties with a series of popular symphonies, choral works and chamber music. Born Arnold Edward Trevor Bax in Streatham, London (November 8, 1883), he studied composition and piano at the Royal Academy of Music. He visited Russia in 1910, an experience that inspired piano pieces 'Gopak' (1911) and 'In A Vodka Shop' (1915). A more important influence was Celtic culture, which informed several orchestral pieces and the choral work *St Patrick's Breastplate* (1923). He also wrote Irish short stories under the name of Dermot O'Byrne. Describing himself as 'a brazen romantic', he wrote seven symphonies, the symphonic poem *Tintagel* (1919), as well as shorter pieces and chamber music. He was knighted in 1937 and in 1942 he was appointed Master of the King's Music. He wrote scores for films including *Oliver Twist* (1948) and also the *Coronation March* for Queen Elizabeth in 1953. He died in Cork, Ireland on October 3, 1953.

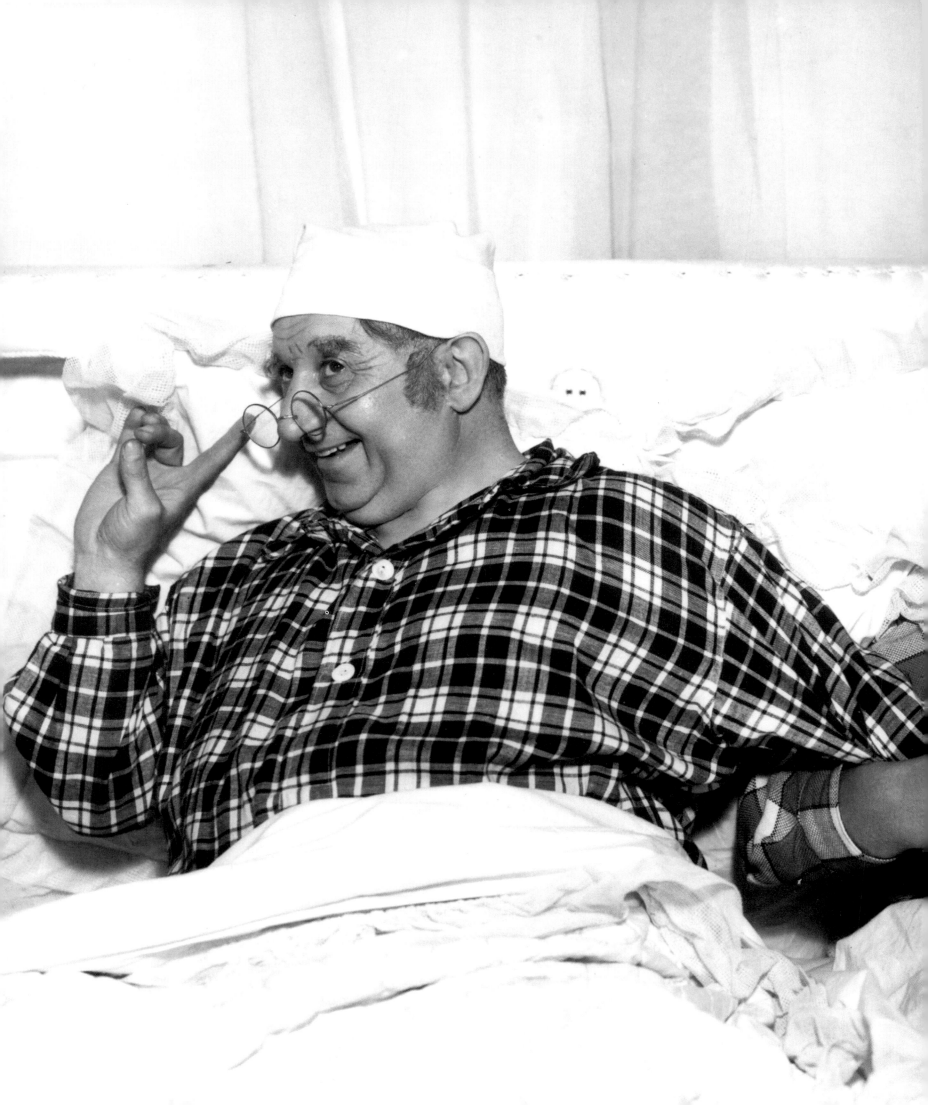

WILL FYFFE

'I belong to Glasgow, dear old Glasgow town'. The working lad who had a couple of drinks on a Saturday found that not only did Glasgow belong to him, but he also had become the toast of the nation, thanks to 'I Belong To Glasgow'. The composer Will Fyffe became one of the most popular music hall acts in the UK in the Thirties and Forties. The songwriter, actor and comedian recorded many of his own witty songs and his biggest hit was even performed by Danny Kaye and Eartha Kitt. Fyffe was born in Dundee, Scotland (February 6, 1885) and made his stage debut aged six with his father's stage company.

He later worked as a character actor starring in many British and Hollywood movies. In 1937 Fyffe appeared at the Royal Command Performance. Following an ear operation he died after a fall from a St Andrews' hotel window on December 14, 1947.

Will Fyffe (left) in bed with music hall legend Bud Flanagan.

ERIC COATES

A generation of British radio listeners and filmgoers have been brought up listening to the stirring marches and soothing melodies of Eric Coates, a much admired composer of light music.

Coates' 'Calling All Workers' (1940) introduced BBC radio's *Music While You Work* that encouraged the nation during World War II and his 'Knightsbridge' from the *London Suite* (1933) heralded the topical *In Town Tonight* show. 'By A Sleepy Lagoon' (1930) is still used as the signature tune for the BBC's *Desert Island Discs*.

Coates, born in Hucknall, Nottinghamshire (August 27, 1886), studied in Nottingham and at the Royal Academy of Music in London. He worked regularly as a viola player with chamber groups until 1912 when he joined the Queen's Hall Orchestra, under Sir Henry Wood. Coates gave up viola to concentrate on composing such works as *The Three Bears* (1926), *Four Centuries* (1941) and *The Three Elizabeths* (1944). He wrote the 'BBC Television March' in 1946 but is best remembered for the iconic 'Dambusters March' featured in the 1954 hit movie.

SIR CHARLES SPENCER 'CHARLIE' CHAPLIN

Music played a vital role in the life and times of cinema's greatest personality, the film comedy actor and director known to the world as Charlie Chaplin. While his iconic creation 'The Tramp' was a key figure in the silent film era, music was important in creating his stories and characters and more so with the introduction of sound. Chaplin was an accomplished musician and film score composer and wrote songs that would become chart hits during the pop era.

He was born in Kennington, London (1889), his mother was a music hall performer and his father a singer. Making his first stage appearance aged five, Chaplin began his career in music hall. Joining Fred Karno's comedy company, he met Debussy in Paris, who complimented the 20 year old on his instinctive musicality.

Chaplin toured America for a second time in 1912 and remained there. Self-taught, he played piano, violin and cello, practising violin for up to six hours a day.

In 1916 Chaplin set up a short-lived publishing company for songs he had written. In 1925 he recorded theme songs composed to coincide with his seminal silent film *The Gold Rush*. When sound arrived, he composed romantic music to contrast with his 'Tramp' character and act as counterpoint to comedy, working with arrangers and orchestrators who scored the ideas he played at the piano for *City Lights* (1931).

Thereafter he wrote scores for all his films including *The Great Dictator* (1940). Among Chaplin's most popular songs were 'Smile' a tune from *Modern Times* (1936), released as a song in 1954 with lyrics by Geoffrey Parsons and John Turner, when it became a hit for Nat King Cole and 'Terry's Theme' from *Limelight* (1952), a hit for Jimmy Young as 'Eternally' (1953) with lyrics by Geoffrey Parsons. 'This Is My Song' from Chaplin's *A Countess From Hong Kong* was a No. 1 UK hit for Petula Clark in 1976. The *Limelight* theme won an Academy Award for Best Original Score after the film's first California re-release in 1972.

Chaplin was knighted by the queen in 1975 and died at his home in Switzerland in 1977.

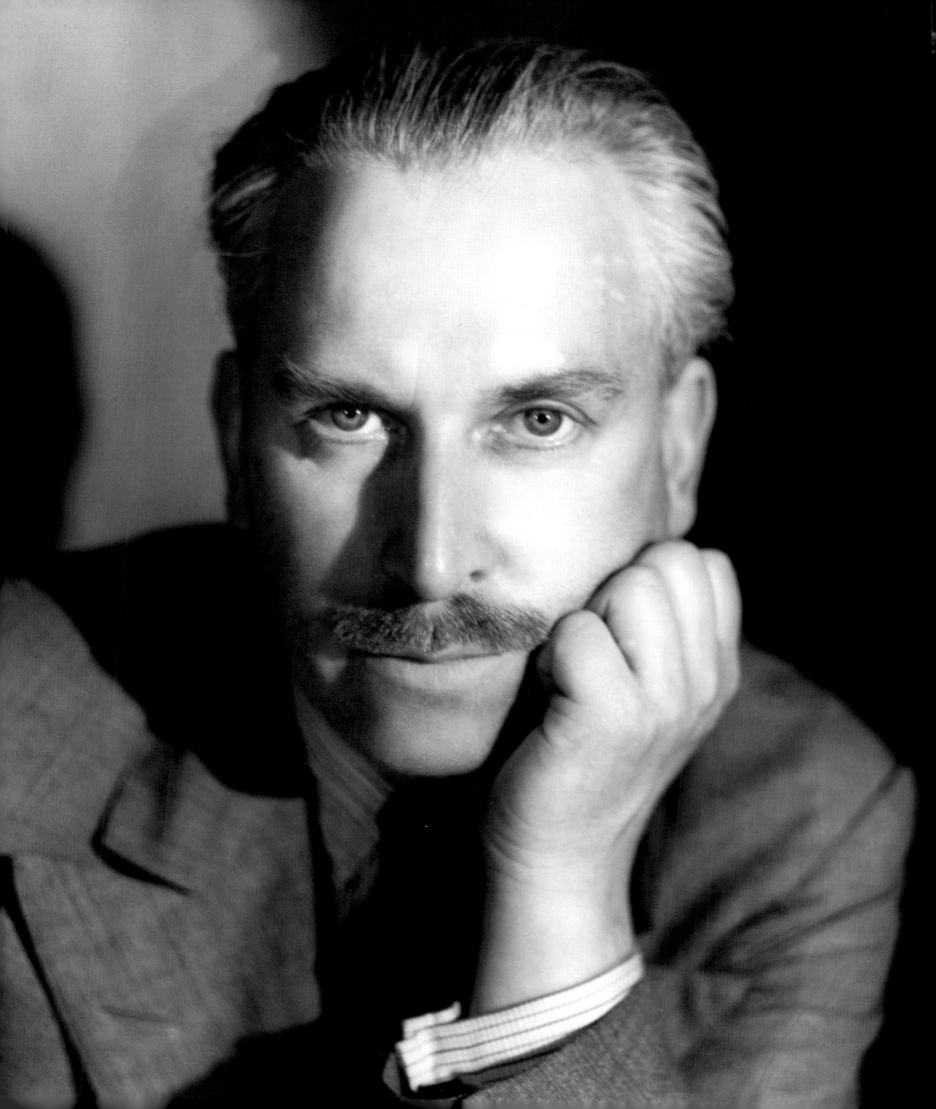

SIR ARTHUR BLISS CH

Composer and conductor Sir Arthur Edward Drummond Bliss, CH (born in London, August 2, 1891), was hailed as a shining light of British music. At Cambridge he studied under Wood and Dent, then with Stanford at the Royal College of Music, and he also received encouragement from Elgar. He served in World War I with distinction, and after 1918 attracted critical attention with several modernist works. During the Twenties his music matured to embrace a characteristic vein of lyrical Romanticism. From 1942 to 1944 he was director of music at the BBC and in 1953 became Master of the Queen's Music. He wrote the music for Alexander Korda's 1936 film *Things To Come* (based on H.G. Wells' novel), the ballets *Checkmate* (1937) and *Miracle In The Gorbals* (1944), the opera *The Olympians* (1949), a choral symphony *Morning Heroes* (1930), the orchestral *A Colour Symphony* (1922), as well as chamber, choral and instrumental works.

He was knighted in 1950 and was president of the Performing Right Society from 1954 to 1975. He died aged 83 (March 27, 1975).

IVOR NOVELLO

In the world of British cultural achievement, Ivor Novello is cherished for his outstanding contributions as an actor, composer, songwriter and dramatist. A star of early silent movies, an icon of West End theatre and composer of the nation's best-loved romantic songs, his name is celebrated by the Ivor Novello Awards, established in his memory in 1955 and awarded each year by BASCA.

Born Ivor Novello Davies in Cardiff (January 15, 1893), Novello sang at the Welsh Eisteddfods as a boy and was educated at Magdalen College School, Oxford. In 1914 he wrote the music to 'Keep The Home Fires Burning', hugely popular during World War I. Other hits included 'And Her Mother Came Too' and 'We'll Gather Lilacs In The Spring'. He debuted on the London stage in 1921 and in 1926 played the lead role in Alfred Hitchcock's silent thriller *The Lodger*. Novello wrote and acted in a series of musicals, notably *Glamorous Nights* (1935), *The Dancing Years* (1939) and *King's Rhapsody* (1949). He died age 58 on March 6, 1951 fêted by peers and public alike.

SIR NOËL COWARD

Gifted with a strong sense of satirical humour and famed for his sharply witty dialogue, Noël Coward achieved international fame as the quintessential Englishman during a glittering career as an actor, singer, dramatist, composer and film producer. His amusing 'Mad Dogs And Englishmen' (1932) became one of his most enduring hits. Born in Teddington, Middlesex (December 16, 1899), Coward made his stage debut in *The Goldfish* in 1911. He wrote his first play in 1920 and went on to create *The Vortex* (1924), *Hay Fever* (1925), *Private Lives* (1930), *Blithe Spirit* (1941) and *This Happy Breed* (1943). Coward was hailed by theatregoers and the acting fraternity as 'The Master'. He wrote and produced many films, notably the award-winning *In Which We Serve* and the much-loved *Brief Encounter*.

After the war he gained popularity in America as a cabaret performer singing 'Alice Is At It Again', 'Uncle Harry' and 'A Room With A View'. The album *Noël Coward At Las Vegas* was a best seller. Knighted in 1969, Sir Noël died on March 26, 1973. In 2006 the former Albery Theatre, London was renamed the Noël Coward Theatre in his honour.

JIMMY KENNEDY OBE

'Red Sails In The Sunset' and 'South Of The Border' are just two of the thousands of songs composed by lyricist Jimmy Kennedy. Born in Omagh, Northern Ireland (July 20, 1902), he began writing songs and poems inspired by Ireland's beautiful scenery. Graduating from Trinity College, Dublin he joined Bert Feldman (the London music publisher) and produced 2000 songs over 50 years. Some 200 were worldwide hits and 50 are viewed as timeless classics.

He served in the Royal Artillery during the war when he wrote 'We're Going To Hang Out The Washing On The Siegfried Line'. He also wrote lyrics to 'My Prayer' and 'Teddy Bears' Picnic' and other hits including 'The Cokey Cokey', 'April In Portugal', 'Istanbul (Not Constantinople)', 'The Isle Of Capri' and 'Love Is Like A Violin'. His songs were performed by artists such as Gracie Fields, Vera Lynn, Perry Como, Fats Domino, Patsy Cline, Tom Jones, Roy Orbison, Frank Sinatra, Elvis Presley and Bing Crosby, who had a hit with 'Did Your Mother Come From Ireland?', a Michael Carr/Kennedy collaboration.

Hugh Williams' 'Harbour Lights' with lyrics by Jimmy Kennedy was a transatlantic hit three times, having been a million-seller for Frances Langford in 1937. It was a US No. 1 by the Sammy Kaye Orchestra in 1950 and a Top 10 US hit for the Platters in 1960. Kennedy songs were also performed by the great big bands led by Ray Noble, Glenn Miller, Herb Alpert and many more.

Kennedy won two Ivor Novello Awards and was awarded the OBE in 1983. He was the chairman of BASCA for 10 years, prior to his death in Cheltenham, England on April 6, 1984. A sculpture in Kennedy's honour was erected on the beach at Portstewart where he had written 'Red Sails In The Sunset'.

SIR LENNOX BERKELEY CBE, OBE

Lennox Berkeley's distinctive compositional style was informed by French and British influences. Born in Oxford (May 12, 1903) and educated at Merton College, Oxford, Berkeley studied music in Paris in 1927 with Nadia Boulanger. In 1936 he met Benjamin Britten at a music festival in Barcelona and they formed a long association, collaborating on the orchestral suite *Mont Juic*. Berkeley's outstanding works composed during World War II include *Serenade For Strings* and Symphony No. 1. In the Forties he unveiled his first Piano Concerto and in 1954 premiered the opera *Nelson* and one-act comedy *A Dinner Engagement*. This was followed by the biblical drama *Ruth* (1956) and a third Piano Concerto (1958). Sir Lennox (who was knighted in 1974) was a professor of composition at the Royal Academy of Music until 1968 and president of the Cheltenham Festival until 1983. He died on December 26, 1989.

GEORGE FORMBY OBE

'Gormless George' comedian, film star, singer and an expert performer on the ukulele was one of Britain's most popular entertainers on stage and screen. His saucy comic songs, delivered with a broad Lancashire accent and cheeky grin, amused audiences for decades. Among his greatest admirers were Beatle George Harrison and comedian Frank Skinner. Born George Hoy Booth in Wigan (May 26, 1904), he was the son of music hall singer James Booth who had performed as 'George Formby'. He originally trained to be a jockey but became a singer after the death of his father. He married Beryl Ingham in 1924. She became his manager and helped the new 'George Formby' to fame. George's 'With My Little Stick Of Blackpool Rock', 'When I'm Cleaning Windows' and 'Leaning On A Lamp Post' were featured on hit records and movies throughout the Thirties and Forties. Formby suffered a heart attack and died on March 6, 1961. Over 100,000 mourners attended his funeral.

VIVIAN ELLIS

'Coronation Scot', that depicted the sound of a steam locomotive gathering speed, became the familiar signature tune for the BBC's *Paul Temple* radio series. It was one of many popular orchestral compositions by Vivian Ellis (born in Hampstead, London, October 29, 1904). After attending Cheltenham College he started his career as a concert pianist. As a composer and lyricist he enjoyed early success with the Twenties foxtrot 'Over My Shoulder'. He also wrote 'Yale Blues', whose dance step the 'Yale' proved a hit in America. Ellis wrote music for West End shows well into the Fifties. Among his best-known songs were 'Spread A Little Happiness' and 'This Is My Lovely Day'. He became president of the Performing Right Society and their annual Vivian Ellis Prize encouraged young composers to write for the stage. His musical *Mr Cinders*, featuring 'Spread A Little Happiness', was revived in London and Sting performed the song in the film *Brimstone And Treacle*. Ellis passed away on June 19, 1996.

SIR MICHAEL TIPPETT OM, CH, CBE

Among the best-known works of Sir Michael Kemp Tippett, a major British composer of the 20th century, are the oratorio *A Child Of Our Time* and the opera *The Midsummer Marriage*.

Michael Tippett (1905–1998) decided on a musical career while a pupil of Stamford School in Lincolnshire, going on to attend the Royal College of Music at two separate periods. He later studied conducting with Malcolm Sargent and Adrian Boult. During World War II he served two months in prison for refusing assigned duties as a conscientious objector.

The Jungian dichotomy of 'shadow and light' was a theme of Tippett's music after he underwent psychoanalysis in the Thirties. Tippett composed some of the most beautiful music for string orchestra since Vaughan Williams, including the *Concerto For Double String Orchestra* (1938–39) and *Fantasia Concertante On A Theme Of Corelli* (1953). Later works showed jazz influences after he visited the US in the Sixties. His five operas challenge conventional expectations. His symphonies, quartets and piano sonatas are part of the core repertoire. His legacy is that of a questioning and enquiring spirit.

A champion of musical education, Tippett was appointed CBE in 1959, made an Honorary Fellow of the Royal College of Music in 1961 and knighted in 1966. Cambridge was among the many universities to award him an honorary doctorate.

PADDY ROBERTS

Prolific composer of hit songs and risqué comic novelty numbers, singer/songwriter Paddy Roberts was much in demand throughout the Fifties. He provided lyrics for many of the best-known artists of the post-war era, contributed to film scores and enjoyed success with his own albums, notably *Strictly For Grown Ups* (1959).

Born John Godfrey Owen Roberts (in Durban, South Africa, 1910), he trained to be a lawyer. During World War II, he joined the RAF as a pilot. As a singer and songwriter he contributed lyrics to Anne Shelton's 1956 UK No. 1 'Lay Down Your Arms'. He also co-wrote Ruby Murray's chart topper 'Softly Softly' (1955) and contributed to 'Pickin' A Chicken', a hit for Eve Boswell (1954). In later years Cilla Black covered his song 'Follow Me'.

His comic numbers include 'The Belle Of Barking Creek' and 'The Tattooed Lady'. He received four Ivor Novello Awards for songwriting and one for services to the British music industry. Paddy died in Dartmouth, Devon in August, 1975.

RONALD BINGE

Much admired for his delightful *Elizabethan Serenade* and *Sailing By*, Binge was a composer of innovative light music popular throughout his lifetime and beyond. Born in Derby (July 15, 1910), he sang in a local church choir as a child. Later a cinema organist, he performed at seaside resorts. He also played organ with the first band led by conductor Mantovani. Binge served in the RAF during the war and helped organise camp entertainments. After the war, Mantovani employed him as arranger and composer for his new orchestra. His arrangement of *Charmaine* using a cascading strings effect resulted in an international hit for Mantovani. Binge also composed original works and film scores. *Elizabethan Serenade* (1951) was used by the BBC as a signature tune, performed in a vocal version as 'Where The Gentle Avon Flows' and also won an Ivor Novello Award. *Sailing By* (1963) regularly introduced the BBC's shipping forecast. Other works include *The Watermill* (1958) and his Symphony in C ('Saturday Symphony', 1970). Binge died in Hampshire aged 69 on September 6, 1979.

BENJAMIN BRITTEN (BARON BRITTEN) OM, CH

Edward Benjamin Britten was one of the UK's most fêted composers as well as being a distinguished conductor and pianist. His prolific output included operas, concertos, choral pieces and orchestral symphonies. Born in Aldeburgh, Suffolk (November 22, 1913), he studied piano and composition before winning a scholarship to the Royal College of Music. Britten first drew attention with the choral work *A Boy Was Born* (1934) and during the Thirties he supplied incidental music for plays and films, often collaborating with W. H. Auden.

He gained international fame with his first opera *Peter Grimes* (1945), while *The Young Person's Guide To The Orchestra* and *Spring Symphony* were also major successes. He wrote two more large-scale operas, *Billy Budd* and *Gloriana* (the latter for Her Majesty The Queen's Coronation), and a series of chamber operas including *The Turn Of The Screw*. Among his later works were *A Midsummer Night's Dream* (1960) and *Death In Venice* (1973). In 1948 he founded the Aldeburgh Festival and, among other honours, he was awarded a life peerage in the year of his death (December 4, 1976). In 2013 Britten's centenary was commemorated with a nationwide series of concerts, broadcasts and TV programmes.

SIR MALCOLM ARNOLD CBE

One of the great composers of the 20th century, Sir Malcolm wrote symphonies, operas, ballet music, film scores, chamber music, music for brass, choral music and over 20 concertos. Born in Northampton (October 21, 1921), he won a scholarship to the Royal College of Music aged 16, and studied trumpet and composition. From 1943 to 1948 he was principal trumpet player with the London Philharmonic Orchestra. After the war he concentrated on composition and conducting. He wrote scores for movies, notably *The Bridge On The River Kwai* (for which he won an Oscar), *The Inn Of The Sixth Happiness* (which won him an Ivor Novello Award), *Whistle Down The Wind* and *David Copperfield*. In 1969 he conducted a Concerto For Group And Orchestra composed by Jon Lord and performed by Deep Purple and the Royal Philharmonic Orchestra at the Royal Albert Hall. In 1986 Sir Malcolm composed his Symphony No. 9. He received an Ivor Novello Award for Outstanding Services to Music in 1986 and a knighthood in 1993. In 2004 he was honoured with the Incorporated Society of Musicians' Distinguished Musician Award 'for his lifetime's achievements as one of the greatest composers of the 20th century'. When he died aged 84 (September 23, 2006), the BBC described him as 'a towering figure in the history of British music'.

RON GOODWIN

One of the UK's finest composers of music for films, Ron Goodwin enjoyed three decades of success during the 20th century. Best remembered for his stirring themes for war films *Where Eagles Dare*, *Battle Of Britain*, *633 Squadron* and *Operation Crossbow*, Goodwin was also a prolific arranger and conductor, responsible for hundreds of hit recordings by dozens of artists. He led his own concert orchestra and was a guest conductor with other world-renowned orchestras.

Born in Plymouth, Devon (February 17, 1925), Ronald Alfred Goodwin played piano from age five. After grammar school he studied trumpet at the Guildhall School of Music. Joining Campbell Connelly as a copyist and arranger, Goodwin began writing scores for dozens of films, worked with producer George Martin at Parlophone and arranged and conducted recordings for over 50 artists on 100 chart hits. He won three Ivor Novello Awards, including a Lifetime Achievement Award. He died aged 77 at his home in Berkshire (January 8, 2003).

HERBERT KRETZMER OBE

The man who wrote the words of the longest running musical in West End history was also a lyricist for *That Was The Week That Was*, the groundbreaking satirical Sixties TV show. Kretzmer was born in Kroonstad, South Africa (October 5, 1925) into a family of Lithuanian immigrants. In the Forties he moved from writing newsreel commentaries to print journalism. Relocating to Fleet Street, he had a successful career with national newspapers and was voted TV Critic of the Year (1980) during a stint with the *Daily Mail*.

His lyrics for musicals and hit songs included 'Goodness Gracious Me' for Peter Sellers and Sophia Loren and 'She' for Charles Aznavour. Cameron Mackintosh asked Kretzmer to write the English version of *Les Misérables* and, despite mixed reviews from fellow critics, 'Les Mis' went on to break records and spawned the hit song 'I Dreamed A Dream'.

Recent work includes *Marguerite*, a musical about Nazi-occupied Paris (music by Michel Legrand, 2008), and *Kristina* about Swedish emigrants to Minnesota in the 19th century (with Benny Andersson and Björn Ulvaeus, 2009). In 1998 Kretzmer was elected a Chevalier of L'Ordre Des Arts Et Des Lettres and took Tony and Grammy Awards for *Les Misérables*. Among other honours, he was given an OBE in 2011.

Photograph by Lucy Sewill, Herbert Kretzmer's home, October 29, 2013.

SIR JOHN DANKWORTH CBE

Bandleader, alto saxophonist, composer and arranger, John Dankworth was one of the most creative figures of the post-war British modern jazz scene. He enjoyed hit records, led a highly popular big band and formed a winning partnership with his wife, singer Cleo Laine. Dankworth, born in Woodford, Essex (September 20, 1927), had violin and piano lessons before studying clarinet and alto saxophone. After study at the Royal Academy of Music, he launched a career as a jazz musician. At the 1949 Paris Jazz Festival he played alongside Charlie Parker and toured with Sidney Bechet. The Dankworth Seven was formed in 1950 and his first big band came in 1953, scoring Top 10 hit singles with 'Experiments With Mice' (1956) and 'African Waltz' (1961). Cleo Laine was the band's vocalist and John and Cleo were married in 1958. Dankworth also composed film and TV scores, notably for *The Avengers* and *Tomorrow's World*. He was knighted in 2006. Sir John was taken ill in 2009 and died aged 82 on February 6, 2010.

LIONEL BART

Composer and lyricist for a string of hit shows, Lionel Bart was acclaimed for his role in reviving the British stage musical during the late Fifties. Among his greatest successes were *Fings Ain't Wot They Used T'be* and *Lock Up Your Daughters* (1959) and *Oliver!* (1960). He also provided hit songs for pop stars and was regarded as a genius, even though he could not read or write music. Born Lionel Begleiter in Stepney, London (August 1, 1930), as a child he showed promise as a painter. Aged 14 he went to St Martins School of Art. After serving in the RAF he became a songwriter and joined Joan Littlewood's Theatre Workshop. He wrote pop songs for Larry Parnes' artists, including Tommy Steele's 'Rock With The Caveman' and Cliff Richard's first No. 1 'Living Doll'. He also wrote 'From Russia With Love' for the James Bond 1963 film. His greatest success came with *Oliver!*, a London stage musical and Oscar-winning movie (1968). It was also a hit on Broadway with such songs as 'As Long As He Needs Me' and 'Consider Yourself'.

Bart received an Ivor Novello Award in recognition of his achievements in 1986, and *Oliver!* was revived at the London Palladium in 1994, with the composer's blessing, to huge commercial success. He died aged 68 on April 3, 1999.

LESLIE BRICUSSE & ANTHONY NEWLEY

The songwriting and theatrical partnership of Leslie Bricusse and Anthony Newley produced some of the most unusual and yet classic hit songs and shows of the early Sixties. The Grammy Award-winning 'What Kind Of Fool Am I?' was just one of Bricusse and Newley's greatest hits. It was a Top 40 success for actor, singer/songwriter and movie star Newley in 1961 and the song also launched Sammy Davis, Jr into the UK charts.

Although long associated with Newley, composer, lyricist and playwright Bricusse (born in London, January 29, 1931) worked with many other artists and composers. He started his theatrical career as secretary of the Cambridge Footlights in 1952. He wrote *Stop The World – I Want To Get Off* together with Newley in 1961, the show yielding 'Once In A Lifetime' as well as 'What Kind Of Fool Am I?'.

Anthony Newley (born in Hackney, London, September 24, 1931) was a child actor who played the Artful Dodger in David Lean's film *Oliver Twist* (1948). His role as a rock 'n' roll singer in *Idol On Parade* (1959) launched him as a real-life pop star with a dozen Top 40 hits and two No. 1 singles – 'Why' and 'Do You Mind' (1960). Newley also wrote the lyrics with Leslie Bricusse for John Barry's *Goldfinger* theme. A major figure in West End theatre, he also recorded many successful solo albums and launched his own surreal ATV show *The Strange World Of Gurney Slade* in 1960. He was inducted into the Songwriters Hall of Fame in 1989.

Leslie Bricusse had stage hits with *Pickwick* (1963), *The Roar Of The Greasepaint – The Smell Of The Crowd* (1965), *Doctor Dolittle* (1967) and *Scrooge*. A parade of artists gained hits with his songs including Harry Secombe ('If I Ruled The World') and Diana Krall ('When I Look In Your Eyes'). Newley and Bricusse also co-wrote music and lyrics for *Willy Wonka & The Chocolate Factory* (1971), and hits such as 'Feeling Good', covered by Nina Simone, Muse and Michael Bublé. Anthony Newley died after suffering ill health aged 67 on April 14, 1999.

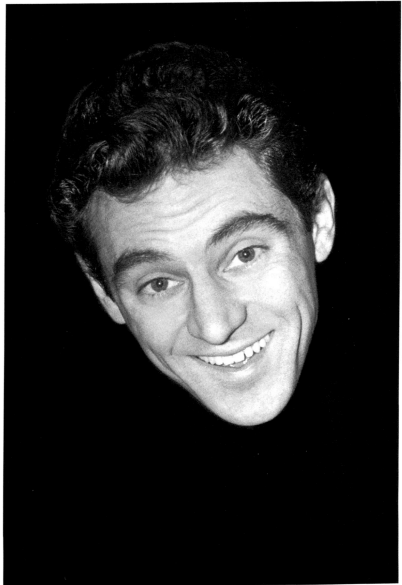

LONNIE DONEGAN (ANTHONY JAMES DONEGAN, MBE)

Lonnie Donegan's influence cannot be overestimated. Bursting into the pop charts in 1956 with 'Rock Island Line', Donegan galvanised the music scene with his energetic brand of skiffle and inspired a whole generation of British youngsters to sing and play in their own skiffle groups. A hugely successful performer, he enjoyed an extraordinary run of 26 Top 20 hit singles, was the first British artist to have an LP enter the charts at No. 1 and the first UK male artist to have two US Top 10 hits. The singer, banjo player and guitarist had emerged from the UK's trad jazz scene to become a popular entertainer, while retaining his roots in American blues and folk music. Born Anthony Donegan in Glasgow (April 29, 1931), he moved to London in 1933. He began to play guitar aged 14 and listened to swing, blues and country records. During the Forties he played guitar in local jazz clubs and joined Chris Barber's jazz band on banjo before being called up for National Service. In 1952 he formed his own band, adopting the name 'Lonnie' inspired by American blues man Lonnie Johnson. While playing with Ken Colyer's outfit, Donegan began singing in a skiffle set during the band's interval using a washboard and tea chest bass. His version of Lead Belly's 'Rock Island Line' was a huge hit at home and in America. Subsequent hits included 'Cumberland Gap', 'Does Your Chewing Gum Lose Its Flavour (On the Bedpost Overnight)' and 'My Old Man's A Dustman'. His successors, The Beatles, Rolling Stones and Elton John, all praised Donegan as an inspiration and in 2000 Lonnie appeared on Van Morrison's album *The Skiffle Sessions*. He died on November 3, 2002 aged 71 following a heart attack.

JOHN BARRY OBE

The winner of five Oscars, four Grammys and many other honours, John Barry OBE created some of the most memorable movie music of all time.

Born John Barry Prendergast (York, 1933) his father owned a chain of cinemas where he became fascinated by both movies and movie music. He played the trumpet and studied music throughout his teens. After National Service, he formed The John Barry Seven, which played rock 'n' roll at various live venues and on TV dance shows such as *Six-Five Special*, *Oh Boy!* and *Drumbeat*. By 1958 his band was backing Adam Faith, and when Faith made his film debut in the 1960 juvenile-delinquent movie *Beat Girl*, it was Barry who supplied its hip jazz-and-rock score. Barry's rapidly growing arranger-producer credits for EMI artists, and his long-held desire to compose on a broader musical canvas soon led to a series of movie assignments.

His work as orchestrator, arranger, conductor and performer of 'The James Bond Theme' in the first 007 film, *Dr. No*, made him the first choice to compose the scores for subsequent films. His bold, brassy and exciting music became a key element of the James Bond formula, scoring 11 Bond films in all. His theme songs were performed by some of the hottest names in popular music, from Shirley Bassey (*Goldfinger*, 1964; *Diamonds Are Forever*, 1971; *Moonraker*, 1979) and Nancy Sinatra (*You Only Live Twice*, 1967) to Duran Duran (*A View To A Kill*, 1985) and his wonderful collaboration with Hal David and Louis Armstrong on the touching love song 'We Have All The Time In The World' for *On Her Majesty's Secret Service* (1969).

Barry also demonstrated a light and lyrical touch for the film *Born Free* (1966), which won him Oscars for Best Song (co-written with Don Black) and Best Score, and the critically acclaimed *The Lion In Winter* (1968) which won him his third Academy Award and the BAFTA Anthony Asquith Award for Original Film Music. He was to win his first Grammy Award for the wistful harmonica theme of John Schlesinger's *Midnight Cowboy* (1969).

Barry's work ranged from stage to screen to television. Having enjoyed a successful London run with the musical *Passion Flower Hotel* in 1965, he collaborated with longtime friend and lyricist Don Black to create another huge West End hit in 1974's *Billy*. His television work included the theme for *The Persuaders!*, *The Glass Menagerie* and *Love Among The Ruins*.

Other important film work included *Out Of Africa* (1985), which won Barry his fourth Academy Award, and *Dances With Wolves* (1990) which earned him a fifth Oscar and a fourth Grammy. His last score was for *Enigma* (2001).

In 1999, Barry was named OBE. In 2001, he received an honorary doctorate from the University of York, and in 2005 became the first composer to receive the BAFTA Fellowship. He died on January 30, 2011 at his home in New York.

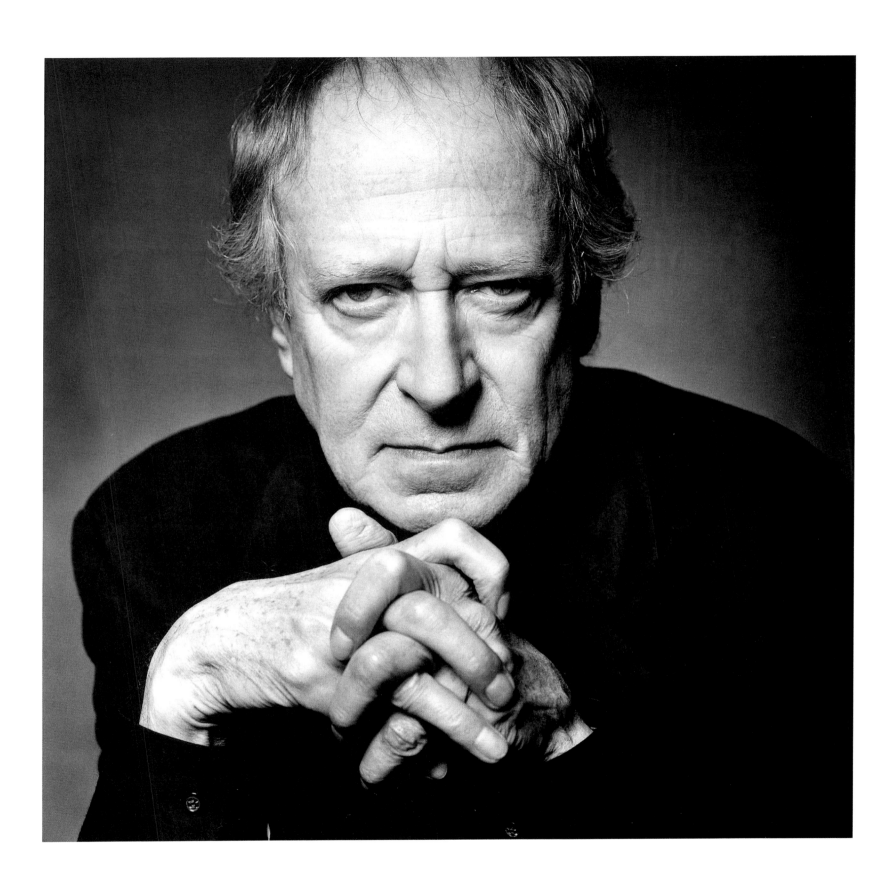

SIR HARRISON BIRTWISTLE CH

'Monumental' and 'dazzling' are among the adjectives critics have used to describe the music of Harrison Birtwistle (born July 15, 1934, Accrington). His orchestral works include *Panic* for solo saxophone, drums and ensemble, which drew a 100 million audience worldwide when it premiered at the 1995 Last Night of the BBC Proms.

While studying clarinet and composition at the Royal Manchester College of Music, he mingled with a creative group of future leading figures including Peter Maxwell Davies and pianist John Ogden. In 1965 he sold his clarinets, having decided to concentrate on composition. A move to Princeton as a Harkness Fellow followed where he completed the opera *Punch And Judy* that established him as a leading British composer. Among his other major works are the Concerto for Violin and Orchestra written for the Boston Symphony Orchestra and his stage works include *The Minotaur* for the Royal Opera and the lyric tragedy *The Mask Of Orpheus*. In the Nineties he composed two operas, including *Gawain*. His work is regularly featured in major festival and concert series. His honours include a Siemens Prize in 1995 and in December 2013 he was presented with his fifth medal at the British Composer Awards for *Gigue Machine* for solo piano. He was knighted in 1988 and made Companion of Honour in 2001.

Major musical events planned for his eightieth birthday during 2014 include a series of Barbican concerts.

Photograph by Lucy Sewill, at Sir Harrison Birtwistle's home, January 30, 2014.

SIR PETER MAXWELL DAVIES CBE, CH

Counted among the leading composers of the day, Peter Maxwell Davies has achieved critical and popular acclaim with his vast canon of work, which includes a 10-symphony cycle described by one critic as the 'most important since Shostakovich'. *The Lighthouse* is arguably his most popular opera, and among his light orchestral works *An Orkney Wedding, With Sunrise*, featuring bagpipes, is one of the most performed pieces of contemporary classical music. Born in Lancashire in 1934, he was part of the New Music Manchester Group as a student. His early works, including *Eight Songs For A Mad King* and others written for the ensemble, The Fires of London, formed by Maxwell Davies and Sir Harrison Birtwistle, gave him a controversial reputation, particularly in the Sixties and Seventies. His move to live in the Orkneys in 1970 was a fundamental source of inspiration in the huge flowering of work from that date on.

His output includes operas (including *Taverner*, *Resurrection* and *Kommilitonen!*), ballets, a series of 10 concertos for the Scottish Chamber Orchestra, a further series of 10 string quartets, commissioned by the recording company Naxos, and many major works for chorus, soloists and orchestra. He has also written film scores and, most importantly, a large body of educational music, reflecting his lifelong concern for music education in both schools and society generally. Maxwell Davies was Associate Composer/Conductor of the BBC Philharmonic and Royal Philharmonic Orchestras, and Composer Laureate with the Scottish Chamber Orchestra. He laid down his baton when he reached 75. He was appointed Master of the Queen's Music in 2004 and his ninth symphony was dedicated to the monarch in her Diamond Jubilee year.

GEOFF STEPHENS

Award-winning composer Geoff Stephens enjoyed a big success with his Grammy Award-winner 'Winchester Cathedral' written in a Twenties style for the New Vaudeville Band in 1966. A surprise US No. 1 for the group he had formed, it was even covered by Dizzy Gillespie and Frank Sinatra.

Geoff (born in Southgate, London, October 1, 1934) wrote songs and sketches for revues while working as a school teacher. His first hit single 'Tell Me When' (1964) was written with Les Reed for the Applejacks, followed by 'The Crying Game' a Top 5 hit for Dave Berry. Geoff collaborated with a string of writers, including John Carter, Roger Greenaway, Peter Callander, Mitch Murray, Barry Mason, Don Black and Tony Macaulay. He also managed and produced the young folk singer Donovan.

Geoff's huge output of songs provided hits for Sixties' stars Manfred Mann, Tom Jones, Cliff Richard, Mary Hopkin, Scott Walker, Wayne Newton, The Drifters and many others. In 1983/84 he composed material for the West End musical *Dear Anyone* with Don Black and for *The Magic Castle* with Les Reed. Geoff was awarded a Gold Badge of Merit by BASCA in 1995 and among his four Ivor Novello Awards, in 2000 he received the Award for Services to British Songwriting.

Photograph by Lucy Sewill, at Geoff Stephens' home, January 29, 2014.

LES REED OBE & BARRY MASON

Les Reed is the man behind a cascade of hit songs that have launched and sustained the careers of dozens of artists and groups. Songwriter, arranger, conductor and orchestra leader, he has worked with several other composers, notably Barry Mason, Gordon Mills, Geoff Stephens, Roger Greenaway, Roger Cook and Sammy Cahn. Born Leslie David Reed in Woking, Surrey (July 24, 1935), he learned to play piano as a five year old and studied at the London College of Music. After National Service and working as a West End nightclub pianist, he joined The John Barry Seven in 1959. After forming a writing partnership with Geoff Stephens, they scored hits with 'Tell Me When' for The Applejacks, 'There's A Kind Of Hush' for Herman's Hermits, as well as 'Daughter Of Darkness' for Tom Jones and 'Baby I Won't Let You Down' for Pickettywitch. In 1972, Elvis Presley took their song 'Sylvia' to the top of the South American charts. In 1964 Reed wrote 'It's Not Unusual' with Gordon Mills, a No. 1 UK hit for Tom Jones. Reed then began working with Barry Mason, creating 'Delilah', another big hit for Tom Jones, among many other hits for various artists.

Barry Mason, born John Barry Mason in Wigan, Lancashire, July 12, 1935 became one of the UK's leading songwriters. After doing his National Service in the Royal Marines he sailed from Liverpool to the US. After lasting one year in Ohio State University he hitch-hiked down Route 66 and spent three years in Hollywood, becoming a resident of the US. He came home to visit his family and decided to give 'showbiz' one more try in London before returning. There began the start of his career. He loved singing and his voice became his instrument to write with.

Barry's first hit was The Merseybeat's 'Don't Turn Around' with Peter Green, soon to be known as Peter Lee Stirling, with whom he later wrote and produced. His main success began with Les Reed, including 'Delilah' and 'I'm Coming Home' for Tom Jones, 'Les Bicyclettes De Belsize' and 'The Last Waltz' for Engelbert Humperdinck, 'Love Is All' for Malcolm Roberts, 'Everybody Knows' for The Dave Clark Five, 'Kiss Me Goodbye' for Petula Clark, 'I Pretend' for Des O'Connor and 'Here It Comes Again' for The Fortunes. Barry has also written for Elvis Presley, Rod Stewart, Barbra Streisand and Gene Pitney.

With Roger Greenaway, Barry wrote 'There Goes My First Love' and 'Can I Take You Home Little Girl' for The Drifters, 'Say You'll Stay Until Tomorrow', a No. 1 country song for Tom Jones and 'You Just Might See Me Cry' for Our Kid.

Barry and Tony Macaulay wrote one of his major hits, 'Love Grows (Where My Rosemary Goes)'. He wrote the English lyrics to two Italian songs, 'A Man Without Love' for Engelbert Humperdinck and 'Love Me Tonight' for Tom Jones and then wrote 'When Forever Has Gone' with Lakis Vlavianos, which broke Demis Roussos in the UK and US. Albert Hammond and Barry wrote the songs for *The Last Horseman*, which premiered in December 2013 in Madrid.

Meanwhile Barry continues to perform his one-man show 'Remember Delilah' all over the world and helps raise funds for many charitable causes.

Barry is very proud to have received five Ivor Novello Awards.

Photograph by Lucy Sewill, at Barry Mason's home, January 15, 2014.

SIR RICHARD RODNEY BENNETT CBE

As one of Britain's most respected and versatile musicians, Bennett produced over 200 works for the concert hall, and 50 scores for film and television, as well as having been a writer and performer of jazz songs for 50 years. Studies with Boulez in the Fifties immersed him in the techniques of the European avant-garde, though he subsequently developed his own distinctive dramato-abstract style. In recent years, he adopted an increasingly tonal idiom. His work with directors John Schlesinger and Sidney Lumet produced scores such as *Murder On The Orient Express*, *Equus*, *Yanks* and *Far From The Madding Crowd*. His parallel career as pianist and singer saw him work with the great singers of our time including Marion Montgomery, Cleo Laine and for the past ten years with Claire Martin with whom he cemented a firm performing and recording relationship.

His contribution to music was recognised both in 1977, when he was appointed a CBE, and in 1998, when he was knighted. He died in New York, aged 76, on Christmas Eve 2012.

DON BLACK OBE

Don Black, songwriter, lyricist, manager and comedian, born Donald Blackstone in Hackney, London (June 21, 1938), has worked with some of the greatest names in the world of music and show business and has been responsible for some of the most memorable and best loved songs in popular music.

Since beginning his career as an office boy and song plugger, he has worked with a 'who's who' of composers including Andrew Lloyd Webber (*Sunset Boulevard*, *Tell Me On A Sunday* and *Aspects Of Love*), Henry Mancini (*The Pink Panther Strikes Again*) and formed a beautiful collaboration with fellow composer John Barry, providing lyrics for Bond songs *Thunderball* (1965), *Diamonds Are Forever* (1971) and *The Man With The Golden Gun* (1974). His biggest success with Barry was with 'Born Free' the title song of the 1966 film, sung by Matt Monro that won an Oscar for Best Song. Don became Matt Monro's personal manager and provided him with lyrics for many more hits. He also worked with Barry on the movies *Out Of Africa* and *Dances With Wolves* and continued the Bond collaboration with David Arnold on songs for *Tomorrow Never Dies* and *The World Is Not Enough*.

In 1969 Black wrote the title song for *The Italian Job* with Quincy Jones. He also wrote 'To Sir With Love', recorded by Lulu and a No. 1 US hit in 1967 for Michael Jackson (who had a US No. 1 with 'Ben').

Don has also received five Academy Award nominations, two Tony Awards, five Ivor Novello Awards and a Golden Globe. In 2007 Don was inducted into the Songwriters Hall Of Fame and in October 2013 a concert to celebrate his life's work was held at the Royal Festival Hall and televised in January 2014.

Photograph of Don Black by Lucy Sewill, at Don's home, January 27, 2014.

ROGER COOK
& ROGER GREENAWAY OBE

C ook and Greenaway, as Roger Cook and Roger Greenaway are known, were the first UK songwriting partnership to be accorded an Ivor Novello Award as Songwriters of the Year for two years running.

Cook (born in Bristol, August 19, 1940), a singer, record producer and songwriter in his own right, met Roger Greenaway when both were members of The Kestrels. In the mid-Sixties, as David and Jonathan, they scored hits including a cover of The Beatles' 'Michelle'.

The Fortunes had success in the UK and US charts with the duo's first hit as songwriters with 'You've Got Your Troubles'. Their other mega hits include 'I'd Like To Teach The World To Sing', 'Melting Pot' and 'Something's Gotten Hold Of My Heart'.

Roger Cook moved to the US in 1975 and later became the first British songwriter to enter the Nashville Songwriters Hall of Fame (1997). Roger Greenaway (born in Bristol, August 23, 1938) stayed in the UK, working with other partners and becoming chairman of the PRS in 1983. He was awarded an OBE for services to the music industry in 1988 and was inducted into the Songwriters Hall of Fame in New York in 2009.

Photograph of Roger Greenaway by Lucy Sewill, at Roger's desk, ASCAP offices, London, December 18, 2014.

BILL MARTIN MBE
& PHIL COULTER

Legendary songwriters Bill Martin and Phil Coulter created timeless pop hits such as 'Puppet On A String' and 'Congratulations' and have received many awards, including a Gold Badge from BASCA in 2009. Martin was born William Wylie Macpherson in Govan, Glasgow on November 9, 1938. Bill Martin originally teamed up in 1963 with Tommy Scott and scored hits for The Bachelors, Twinkle and The Dubliners. In 1965 Martin formed a new partnership with pianist Phil Coulter (born in Derry, Northern Ireland, February 19, 1942). Coulter had arrived from Ireland in 1964 to work in London's Denmark Street as an arranger for The Dubliners, Van Morrison and The Bachelors. Martin and Coulter went on to write the first British Eurovision Song Contest Winner, Sandie Shaw's 1967 chart topper 'Puppet On A String'. In 1968 'Congratulations' was a No. 1 for Cliff Richard and came second in the Eurovision Song Contest that year. Many more Martin and Coulter hits followed, notably for the Bay City Rollers, Cilla Black and Elvis Presley. In 1975 they jointly received an Ivor Novello Award for Songwriter of the Year.

TONY HATCH

Born in Pinner, Middlesex (June 30, 1939), Hatch was educated at the London Choir School until 1955 when he entered the music business as a tea boy in a West End music publishing house. From this humble beginning, his prodigious talent was to take him to the top of the profession. In the early Sixties he wrote and produced records by numerous artists but it was his meeting with Petula Clark that brought him world fame as a songwriter. Their collaboration gave them chart-topping success in the UK and the US with 'Downtown', 'I Know A Place', 'My Love', 'Colour My World', 'I Couldn't Live Without Your Love' and 'Don't Sleep In The Subway'. Tony also wrote 'Sugar And Spice' for The Searchers and 'Forget Him' for Bobby Rydell. Hatch's themes for TV include *Crossroads*, *Neighbours* and *Emmerdale*. He was inducted into the Songwriters Hall of Fame in 2013.

Photograph by Lucy Sewill, Marylebone High Street, London, October 10, 2013.

MITCH MURRAY & PETER CALLANDER

Award-winners Mitch Murray and Peter Callander formed such a successful partnership that they soon became known to their peers as 'star songwriters'. Hits poured from their collective pen for a range of artists from The Tremeloes and Cliff Richard to Manfred Mann, Vanity Fare and Tony Christie. Murray (born in Hove, Sussex, January 30, 1940) worked as a salesman for his father's firm. Learning to play the ukulele on holiday, he began writing songs. During his career in music, he would achieve five UK and three US No. 1s. Early success came with 'How Do You Do It?' recorded by The Beatles (but not released until 1995) and a UK No. 1 for Gerry and The Pacemakers (1963). 'I Like It' also topped the charts for Gerry that year.

'You Were Made For Me' and 'I'm Telling You Now' were more Murray hits, for Freddie and The Dreamers. Following this success, Murray published *How To Write A Hit Song*, a 1964 book that inspired 12-year-old Gordon Sumner (Sting) to write songs.

Murray later teamed up with Peter Callander (born October 10, 1939), with Murray writing the music and Callander providing the lyrics. Their joint hits included 'Even The Bad Times Are Good' (The Tremeloes), 'Goodbye Sam, Hello Samantha' (Cliff Richard), 'Hitchin' A Ride' (Vanity Fare) and 'The Ballad Of Bonnie And Clyde', a 1967 UK No. 1 for Georgie Fame. They also produced Tony Christie's version of Neil Sedaka's 'Is This The Way To Amarillo?' a 1971 Top 20 hit and a UK No. 1 in 2007. Their 'Avenues And Alleyways' was also a hit for Christie in 1971. Murray and Callander then launched Paper Lace, whose 'Billy Don't Be A Hero' was a UK No. 1 in 1974.

As well as co-writes with Murray, Callander penned hits for Dusty Springfield, Cilla Black, Cliff Richard, Tom Jones, Sandie Shaw and Lulu, and scored a No. 1 in the US with Wayne Newton ('Daddy Don't You Walk So Fast'), a collaboration with Geoff Stephens.

In 1968 Murray became the youngest director of the PRS and in 1971 he founded the Society of Distinguished Songwriters. A successful humorous speech writer, he has written best-selling books on the subject. Murray, who remains a PRS board member, has won two Ivor Novello Awards and been awarded a BASCA Gold Badge of Merit. Peter Callander was the recipient of two Ivor Novello Awards and a BASCA Gold Badge, and was a director of PRS and MCPS. He died on February 25, 2014.

Photographs by Lucy Sewill, at Mitch Murray's home, January 31, 2014 and Peter Callander's home, February 2, 2014.

BRIAN BENNETT OBE, BRUCE WELCH OBE & HANK MARVIN

Pivotal members of The Shadows, Bennett and Welch developed parallel careers as producers and songwriters. Bennett, born in Palmers Green, London (February 9, 1940), joined a skiffle group at 16 and later became house drummer at Soho's 2i's coffee bar. He joined Marty Wilde's Wildcats in 1959 and backed Tommy Steele, Gene Vincent and Eddie Cochran. He joined Cliff Richard and The Shadows in 1961 and co-wrote their hit songs, including the Ivor Novello Award-winning 'Summer Holiday' and 'Wonderful Life'. He has since composed more music for films and TV shows, notably for *Birds Of A Feather* and *New Tricks*. He was appointed an OBE in 2004. In 2009 Bennett played with Cliff and The Shadows on their 50th anniversary tour.

Bruce Welch, born in Bognor Regis (November 2, 1941), is a guitarist, composer, producer and music publisher. Growing up in County Durham, he formed the skiffle group the Railroaders aged 14. School friend Hank Marvin joined the group and both lads moved to London in 1958 to join The Drifters, Cliff Richard's backing group, later renamed The Shadows. Welch co-wrote hit numbers for the group such as 'FBI', 'Foot Tapper' and 'The Rise And Fall Of Flingle Bunt', and Cliff's hits 'Please Don't Tease', 'In The Country', 'Bachelor Boy' and 'Summer Holiday'.

Welch produced Cliff's hit album *I'm Nearly Famous* and singles 'Devil Woman' and 'We Don't Talk Anymore', and was a producer for Olivia Newton-John. He was appointed an OBE in 2004.

Hank B. Marvin, born in Newcastle-upon-Tyne (October 28, 1941), as lead guitarist with The Shadows helped define their unique sound and was a strong influence on many of the world's rock guitarists. He has released several instrumental and some vocal albums, notably *Words And Music*, *All Alone With Friends*, *Guitar Player* and *The Hank Marvin Guitar Syndicate*. His *Guitar Man* (2007), featuring songs by Sting, Cat Stevens and George Harrison among others, got to No. 6 in the UK charts. He has co-written several songs for Cliff including 'On The Beach' and 'In The Country' and co-wrote Olivia Newton-John's 1977 hit 'Sam' with John Farrar and Don Black. He has collaborated on albums with Jean Michel Jarre and French guitarist Jean-Pierre Danel and released a swing and gypsy jazz album, *Django's Castle*, with accordionist Nunzio Mondia and guitarist Gary Taylor in 2013.

JOHN LENNON & SIR PAUL McCARTNEY MBE

The success of The Beatles was predicated on the songwriting partnership forever known as Lennon and McCartney. Clever, melodic, original songs flowed during The Beatles' glory years from 1962 to 1970. The friends shared credits from 'Love Me Do' (1962) onwards during an extraordinary career that saw them conquer America as well as make groundbreaking albums and hit movies.

Among the pantheon of Lennon and McCartney classics are 'I Saw Her Standing There', 'PS I Love You', 'There's A Place', 'From Me To You', 'She Loves You', 'All My Loving', 'I Want To Hold Your Hand', 'Can't Buy Me Love', 'Ticket To Ride', 'Yesterday', 'Norwegian Wood', 'Michelle', 'Strawberry Fields Forever', 'Penny Lane', 'When I'm Sixty Four', 'Hey Jude', 'Lady Madonna' and 'The Long And Winding Road'. Not bad for two lads from Liverpool. The Beatles evolved from The Quarrymen skiffle group formed by John Lennon (born October 9, 1940) that later recruited Paul McCartney (born June 18, 1942). After the Beatles ended in 1970 both men embarked on solo careers.

In one of rock's great tragedies, John died at the hands of a gunman in New York City on December 8, 1980. McCartney has continued as a performer and songwriter through turbulent times, honoured and respected by peers and the public alike. He was knighted in 2010.

GEORGE HARRISON MBE

Guitarist, songwriter, singer, producer of music and film, George Harrison grew up in post-war Liverpool listening to the skiffle music of Lonnie Donegan and American rock 'n' roll and playing guitar. Harrison was busy internalising the sounds of Little Richard, Buddy Holly, Elvis Presley, Carl Perkins and other rock 'n' roll pioneers, when in 1958 he joined The Quarrymen, a group founded by John Lennon and including Paul McCartney, both fellow Liverpudlians.

By 1962, The Quarrymen had become The Beatles and added Ringo Starr, and Harrison assumed the role of lead guitarist. Although often described as 'the quiet Beatle', Harrison's guitar style and writing were central to The Beatles' sound. He penned several Beatles hits, including 'Something', 'Taxman', 'While My Guitar Gently Weeps', and 'Here Comes The Sun'. Harrison also developed his musical voice outside of The Beatles: following his immersion in Indian music, he composed and arranged a soundtrack of Indian instrumentals for the film *Wonderwall* (1968), and in 1970 was the first member of The Beatles to release a post-breakup solo album. This release, *All Things Must Pass*, went to the No. 1 position on the UK charts, as did the album's major single, 'My Sweet Lord'. Soon after this, Harrison staged a two-night performance in New York called 'The Concert for Bangla Desh', which became memorable both as an album release featuring an all-star cast of performers and as the first instance of a charity event in rock music.

While continuing to release albums under his own name and collaborating with musicians such as Ravi Shankar, Eric Clapton and Bob Dylan, Harrison formed a record company (Dark Horse Records, in 1974) and a film company (HandMade Films, in 1978). As he pursued his musical interests he also backed a number of successful films, including *Monty Python's Life Of Brian* (1979), *Time Bandits* (1982), and *Brazil* (1984). Harrison continued his musical output through his work with Tom Petty, Jeff Lynne, Roy Orbison, and Bob Dylan as the Traveling Wilburys, as well as his own solo recordings, including *Living In The Material World* (1973), *Somewhere In England* (1981), *Cloud Nine* (1987) and *Live In Japan* (1992).

George Harrison died aged 58 on November 29, 2001. In his final months he had continued to work on songs for *Brainwashed*, a project started many years before, which was to be his final album. Produced by Jeff Lynne and Dhani Harrison, who completed work on the recordings to George's detailed specifications after his death, the record was released to universal acclaim in 2002, with album track 'Marwa Blues' winning a Grammy Award for Best Pop Instrumental Performance in 2004.

MICK JAGGER & KEITH RICHARDS

The Rolling Stones and the world benefited when Jagger and Richards developed their songwriting partnership that resulted in a stream of hits, assuring the group's popularity well into the 21st century. Originally inspired by the R&B of Chuck Berry and Bo Diddley, the Stones evolved into a stylish rock 'n' roll band famed for such blockbusters as '(I Can't Get No) Satisfaction', 'Get Off Of My Cloud', '19th Nervous Breakdown', 'Let's Spend The Night Together', 'Paint It Black', 'Jumpin' Jack Flash', 'Honky Tonk Women', 'Brown Sugar' and 'It's Only Rock And Roll'. The group, founded by Brian Jones in 1962, was fronted by lead singer Michael Philip Jagger, born in Dartford, Kent (July 26, 1943), and powered up by guitarist Keith Richards, also from Dartford (born December 18, 1943) and a friend from childhood. Their shared love of the blues led to a lifelong musical partnership and the creation of riffs, themes and songs filled with revolution, sexual energy and the angst of youth.

ROGER WATERS & DAVID GILMOUR CBE

Roger Waters and David Gilmour, Nick Mason and Richard Wright achieved fame as members of Pink Floyd, selling more than 250 million records worldwide.

Roger Waters (born in Great Bookham, Surrey, September 6, 1943) co-founded Pink Floyd in 1965 with Nick Mason, Richard Wright and Syd Barrett. When Syd left the band, Waters become the principal songwriter. His conceptual approach informed legendary albums, including *The Dark Side Of The Moon*, *Wish You Were Here* and *Animals* as well as the semi-autobiographical *The Wall* before he left the group in 1985. In 1990, he staged *The Wall – Live In Berlin*, one of the largest rock concerts in history. Waters' solo career includes the albums *The Pros And Cons Of Hitch Hiking*, *Radio K.A.O.S.* and *Amused To Death* as well as his opera *Ça Ira*. In 2005 he reunited with Pink Floyd for the Live 8 concert in London. In 2013, Waters concluded a tour of *The Wall Live*, which was the highest grossing tour of all time by a solo artist.

David Gilmour (born in Cambridge, March 6, 1946), a childhood friend of Syd Barrett, became the fifth member of Pink Floyd in 1968, the band reverting to a four-piece on Barrett's departure soon after. David Gilmour's distinctive guitar and vocals feature on 13 of the band's 14 studio albums, including *A Momentary Lapse Of Reason* (1987) and *The Division Bell* (1994). Gilmour has his own unique style of songwriting and collaborated with Waters on many of the band's most iconic songs, including 'Comfortably Numb' and 'Wish You Were Here'. David Gilmour's third solo album, *On An Island*, entered the UK charts at No. 1 on its release in 2006. In the previous year he was awarded a CBE for services to music.

LED ZEPPELIN

JOHN BONHAM
JOHN PAUL JONES
JIMMY PAGE OBE
ROBERT PLANT CBE

The most successful and influential rock group of the Seventies and armed with the expertise of Jimmy Page, Robert Plant, John Paul Jones and John Bonham, Led Zeppelin matched a dynamic live stage act with million-selling albums. Their roots lay in the blues and rock 'n' roll but absorbed other influences including folk, reggae and Arabic music. Plant and Page made a formidable writing team, blending exotic lyrics and masterful guitar playing on 'Stairway To Heaven'. John Paul Jones added creativity as keyboard player, bassist and arranger while Bonham's drumming was all-powerful. Managed by Peter Grant, the band signed to Atlantic in 1968 and unleashed albums packed with classics such as 'Whole Lotta Love', 'Communication Breakdown', 'Dazed And Confused' and 'Kashmir'. The band broke up after the death of John Bonham in 1980, but reformed for special events, notably their final historic concert at London's O$_2$ Arena on December 10, 2007.

SIR JOHN TAVENER

Born in London (January 28, 1944), Tavener was an award-winning student at the Royal Academy of Music. *The Whale* was his first work to gain attention in 1968. But it was not until the premiere of *The Protecting Veil* and the best-selling record of that piece (1992) that Tavener's reputation was assured. Five years later global attention focused on his *Song For Athene* as it closed the funeral service for Diana, Princess of Wales.

John Tavener's works are threaded with streams of metaphysical and musical thought, often with reference to death, world end, paradise and loss of innocence.

Raised a Presbyterian, he was influenced by mystical aspects of Roman Catholicism in the Sixties and Seventies but later converted to Russian Orthodoxy, producing his *Akhmatova Requiem* in 1981. His devout faith drove all his works, but his interest in different belief systems, including those of the East, could be heard in later works such as *The Veil Of The Temple* and *Lament For Jerusalem*. Despite major health problems he continued composing until his death on November 12, 2013. He was knighted in 2000 for his services to music.

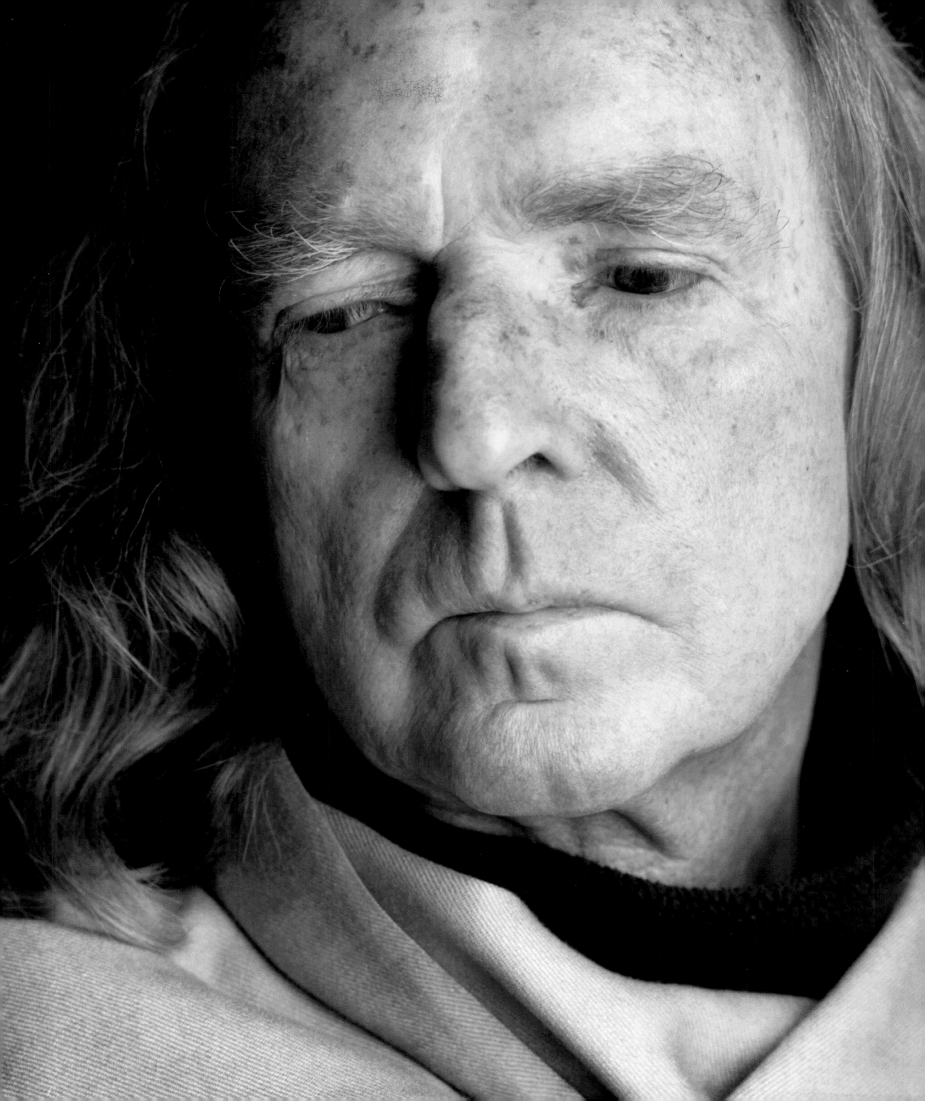

MICHAEL NYMAN CBE

Composer, critic, author and photographer, Michael Nyman has produced a wide range of music during an illustrious career, from film scores to string quartets and operas. A classically trained musician, he absorbed influences from The Beatles to the avant-garde and the work of John Cage. Born in Stratford, London (March 23, 1944), he studied piano and 17th-century baroque music at the Royal Academy of Music. Rebelling against orthodoxy, Nyman spent some years writing music criticism for *The Listener* and *The Spectator*. He later performed with The Flying Lizards and the Portsmouth Sinfonia and played piano on the *20 Classic Rock Classics* album. He has written scores for many films, notably Peter Greenaway's *The Cook, The Thief, His Wife & Her Lover*. His emotive score for Jane Campion's 1993 film *The Piano* resulted in a best-selling classical music soundtrack album and he was nominated for a British Academy Award and a Golden Globe.

ALBERT HAMMOND OBE

Albert Hammond has enjoyed a multifaceted career as a successful artist, songwriter and producer. Born in London (May 18, 1944), his parents returned to their native Gibraltar after World War II. Here Hammond grew up bilingual, his fluent Spanish later enabling him to score hits as a singer/songwriter in Spain as well as the United States and the UK. He began writing a string of hit songs in the Sixties, starting with 'Little Arrows' for Leapy Lee, composed at age 24.

Albert co-founded British vocal group The Family Dogg with fellow vocalist Mike Hazlewood in 1966 and they formed a long-term writing partnership. Their composition 'The Air That I Breathe' gave the Hollies a hit in 1974. Hammond also co-wrote many hits with Diane Warren, notably Chicago's 'I Don't Wanna Live Without Your Love', Starship's 'Nothing's Gonna Stop Us Now' and Roy Orbison's 'Careless Heart'.

Moving to the United States in the Seventies, Albert achieved solo success with 'It Never Rains In Southern California' and since then has written material for a wide range of artists notably Tina Turner, Celine Dion, Whitney Houston, Aretha Franklin, Elton John, Joe Cocker, Diana Ross, Johnny Cash and k.d. lang.

His songs have crossed genres, topping pop, R&B, country and Latin charts and have been responsible for sales of over 360 million records including 30 chart-topping singles. Many of his best-known songs such as 'The Air That I Breathe' and 'When I Need You' have been hits multiple times for different artists.

He has been nominated for several awards and won an Emmy in 1988. In 2000 he was awarded an OBE and was inducted into the Songwriters Hall of Fame in 2008. In 2010 Albert released his album *Legend*, performing some of his greatest compositions with artists including Cliff Richard, Julio Iglesias, Al Stewart and Bonnie Tyler. He also performed a duet with his son Albert Hammond, Jr. His latest album, *Legend II*, was released in 2012.

RAY DAVIES CBE

Founder member of The Kinks, Ray Davies is one of the UK's most original songwriters. His group laid the foundations for heavy rock with 'You Really Got Me'. However, Davies would go on to develop a poignant lyrical style with his songs 'Dedicated Follower Of Fashion', 'Sunny Afternoon' and 'Waterloo Sunset'. Raymond Douglas Davies, born in Muswell Hill, London (June 21, 1944), was an art student before joining brother Dave in The Ravens in 1963, the blues outfit that evolved into The Kinks. Their single 'You Really Got Me' hit No. 1 in the UK chart in 1964. Ray developed his songwriting skills on *(The Kinks Are) The Village Green Preservation Society*, their 1968 album, while 'Lola' and 'Apeman' were both hits in 1970. The Kinks were inducted into the Rock and Roll Hall of Fame in 1990 and received Ivor Novello Awards in 1990. Ray Davies published his autobiography *X Ray* (1994) and in 2004 was awarded a CBE. He performed 'Waterloo Sunset' at the closing ceremony for the London Summer Olympics in 2012.

Photograph by Lucy Sewill, Konk Studios, London, December 17, 2013.

TIM RICE

Tim Rice has worked in music, theatre and films since 1965 when he met Andrew Lloyd Webber, a fellow struggling songwriter. Rather than pursue Tim's ambitions to write rock or pop songs, they turned their attention to Andrew's obsession – musical theatre. Their first collaboration (lyrics by Tim, music by Andrew) was an unsuccessful show based on the life of Dr. Barnardo, the Victorian philanthropist, *The Likes Of Us*. Their next three works together were much more successful: *Joseph And The Amazing Technicolor Dreamcoat*, *Jesus Christ Superstar* and *Evita*. Tim has also worked with other distinguished popular composers such as Elton John (*The Lion King*, *Aida*), Alan Menken (*Aladdin*, *King David*, *Beauty And The Beast*), Björn Ulvaeus and Benny Andersson (*Chess*) and most recently, Stuart Brayson (*From Here To Eternity*).

He formed his own cricket team in 1973 and was president of the MCC in 2002. In 2010–11 he wrote and presented a 52-part series for BBC Radio 2, *American Pie*, a trawl through the music and musicians of every American State. He has won several awards, mainly for the wrong thing or for simply turning up.

Photograph by Lucy Sewill, at Tim Rice's home, December 2, 2013.

10cc

LOL CRÈME
KEVIN GODLEY
GRAHAM GOULDMAN
ERIC STEWART

Art rock group 10cc was founded in 1972 by four multi-instrumentalists, three of them childhood friends from the Manchester area. The band was formed after Hotlegs, who had a UK Top 5 hit with 'Neanderthal Man' (1970) and featured Eric Stewart (vocals, guitar), Lol Crème (vocals, guitar) and Kevin Godley (vocals, drums), were joined by Graham Gouldman (vocals, bass).

Gouldman and Stewart specialised in writing commercial pop songs, while Godley and Crème injected an experimental edge to the band with their compositions. Eventually this duality was seen as a problem rather than an asset and led to the band splitting in 1976.

Their first hit 'Donna' got to No. 2 in the UK chart in 1972, followed by chart topper 'Rubber Bullets' that led to a US tour in 1974. Further self-produced hits on the UK label and recorded at Stockport's Strawberry Studios included 'The Dean And I', 'The Wall Street Shuffle', 'Silly Love' and 'Life Is A Minestrone', performances critically acclaimed for their wit and sophistication.

Debut album *10cc* (1973) was followed by *Sheet Music* (1974), then in 1975 10cc signed to Mercury Records. The group achieved a major hit with the enduring 'I'm Not In Love', a UK No. 1 in May 1975, which reached No. 2 on the US Billboard chart and No. 1 on the Cashbox chart. The ballad had been featured on *The Original Soundtrack* (1975) album, which also included 'mini-operetta' 'Une Nuit A Paris'. The band's fourth album *How Dare You!* (1976) was followed by *Bloody Tourists* (1978). Further Top 10 hit singles included 'Art For Art's Sake', 'I'm Mandy Fly Me', 'The Things We Do For Love', 'Good Morning Judge' and UK No. 1 'Dreadlock Holiday'.

Godley and Crème left 10cc in 1976 while Gouldman and Stewart remained. After pursuing many individual projects in the Eighties, the four original members reunited in 1991 to record a new album…*Meanwhile*.

ERIC CLAPTON CBE, OBE

Eric 'Slowhand' Clapton (born in Ripley, Surrey, March 30, 1945) is the only three-time inductee to the Rock and Roll Hall of Fame (as a solo artist and as a member of both The Yardbirds and Cream). Given a cheap guitar aged 13, Clapton started out as a street busker. He joined The Yardbirds in 1963 but quit, claiming they were moving away from the blues. Recruited by John Mayall's Blues Breakers in 1965, his reputation soared as a masterful blues guitarist and 'Clapton is God' appeared on street graffiti. In 1966 he formed Cream with Ginger Baker and Jack Bruce, and powerful instrumental solos and hit records such as 'Sunshine Of Your Love' won great success in the US. Blind Faith followed in 1969, then came his group Derek and The Dominos and their classic song 'Layla'. Clapton's first No. 1 vocal hit was a cover of Bob Marley's 'I Shot The Sheriff' but he also developed as a songwriter, composing such classics as 'Layla', 'Wonderful Tonight' and 'Tears In Heaven'.

During a 50-year career, Clapton has collaborated with many top artists, notably Bob Dylan, Phil Collins, George Harrison and Roger Waters. His accolades include 17 Grammy Awards, a Brit Award for Outstanding Contribution to Music, an OBE (1994) and CBE (2004).

MIKE CHAPMAN & NICKY CHINN

Mike Chapman and Nicky Chinn were unassailable during the glam rock era. The songwriting team were responsible for a string of huge hits for many of the greatest acts of the Seventies, notably Sweet, Mud, Smokie and Suzi Quatro. Lively, fun and dynamic, their lyrics and tunes invigorated the charts and furthered the careers of dozens of artists.

Michael 'Mike' Chapman (born in Queensland, Australia, April 13, 1947) emigrated to the UK, where he joined the group Tangerine Peel before teaming up with Nicky Chinn after meeting in a London club.

They began writing in 1970, having joined up with Mickie Most, head of RAK Records, and the hits soon followed for the team dubbed 'Chinnichap'.

With 19 Top 40 UK singles during 1973/74, including five No. 1s, at one point a quarter of all the singles sold in the UK were Chapman and Chinn songs, including Sweet's 'Blockbuster', 'Ballroom Blitz' and 'Teenage Rampage', and Mud's 'Dynamite', 'Tiger Feet' and their 1974 No. 1 'Lonely This Christmas'. Suzi Quatro's Chinnichap successes included 'Can The Can', '48 Crash' and 'Devilgate Drive', Smokie's many hits included the worldwide success 'Living Next Door To Alice' and the partnership also had huge US successes with Exile's 'Kiss You All Over' in 1978, Toni Basil's 'Mickey' in 1982, Huey Lewis & The News' 'Heart And Soul' and Tina Turner's 'Better Be Good To Me' (co-written with Holly Knight) amongst others.

Nicky Chinn (born in London, May 16, 1945) had developed a talent for songwriting as a young man, beginning with songs for the film *There's A Girl In My Soup* (1970), co-written with singer Michael d'Abo. Once teamed up with Mike Chapman, a torrent of hits flowed. They split up in 1983, but during their 12 years together they had co-written over 50 Top 40 hits. During their careers they received three Ivor Novello Awards including the 1997 Jimmy Kennedy Award for outstanding career achievement. Nicky more recently wrote 'You Must Have Had A Broken Heart' with Jörgen Elofsson for Westlife's UK No. 1 album *Back Home*, co-wrote 'Live Like There's No Tomorrow' for Selena Gomez's 2010 album *A Year Without Rain* and 'A Beautiful Life' for Donny and Marie Osmond for their 2010 album *Donny And Marie*.

Mike Chapman moved to America in 1975 where he produced 'Kiss You All Over' for Exile, 'Hot Child In The City' for Nick Gilder and devised the Knack's multi-million selling US and worldwide No. 1 'My Sharona'. He co-wrote Pat Benatar's 'Love Is A Battlefield' and both Tina Turner's anthem 'The Best' and 'In Your Wildest Dreams' (all with Holly Knight). He produced four albums for Blondie, commencing with *Parallel Lines*, each yielding hit singles, notably 'Sunday Girl', 'Hanging On The Telephone', 'Heart Of Glass', 'One Way Or Another', 'Dreaming', 'Atomic', 'Rapture', 'The Tide Is High', 'Island Of Lost Souls' and 'War Child'. He has also produced albums and singles for artists including Tina Turner, Rod Stewart, Lita Ford, Ozzy Osborne, Altered Images and Bow Wow Wow. Most recently Chapman has worked with Haim, FKA Twigs and newcomers Lisa Watchorn and Purple Apple.

PETE TOWNSHEND

Godfather of The Who, Pete Townshend remains rock music's great innovator and eloquent spokesperson. As a composer, he readily captured the rebellious mood of Sixties youth, articulating their feelings with the exhilarating songs 'I Can't Explain', 'Anyway, Anyhow, Anywhere', 'My Generation' and 'Substitute'. Encouraged by The Who's manager Kit Lambert, who proudly described Townshend as 'a genius', the guitarist, singer and composer further developed ideas with extended work 'A Quick One While He's Away' (1966) and the rock opera *Tommy* (1969). The latter album, featuring 'Pinball Wizard', was a huge success for The Who and became the basis for a major film. Townshend, born in Chiswick, London (May 19, 1945), is also a dynamic guitarist and recording expert. *Who's Next* (1971) and *Quadrophenia* (1973) further revealed his creative powers, with the latter also being made into a successful film. Townshend, who released several solo albums including *Who Came First* (1972), *Empty Glass* (1980) and *Psychoderelict* (1993), sustained the legacy of The Who following the death of Keith Moon (1978) and published his revealing autobiography *Who I Am* in 2012.

VAN MORRISON OBE

Poetic mystic and gravel-voiced soul singer, Van Morrison has achieved greatness during a lifetime of achievement. In 2013 he was given the freedom of the City of Belfast, one of a long list of awards and accolades heaped on 'The Belfast Cowboy' during a career that began with a skiffle group when he was aged 12.

Born George Ivan Morrison in Belfast, Northern Ireland (August 31, 1945), he sang and played saxophone with a showband before becoming lead singer with R&B group Them in 1963. Success came when 'Baby Please Don't Go' backed by Morrison's own composition 'Gloria' and a version of Bert Berns' 'Here Comes The Night' were both chart hits in 1965. After Them split in 1966, Morrison recorded 'Brown Eyed Girl', a US Top 10 hit. Next came the mystical song cycle *Astral Weeks* (1968) and *Moondance* (1970), both acclaimed by the critics as rock milestones. His unique musical style developed from an early appreciation of blues and jazz blended with a growing interest in the healing power of music and poetry. Morrison released his 34th studio album *Born to Sing: No Plan B* in 2012.

THE BEE GEES

BARRY GIBB CBE
MAURICE GIBB CBE
ROBIN GIBB CBE

Barry Gibb formed the Bee Gees along with his younger twin brothers Maurice and Robin in 1958. They would go on to become one of the biggest-selling bands of all time.

Commemorative stamps have been issued honouring them on the Isle of Man, their birthplace, and in 2013 surviving Bee Gee Barry unveiled a statue of them in Australia, where they made their first records.

Moving to England in the late Sixties, they were supported by producer Robert Stigwood and their career soared. Their success was founded on songwriting versatility and distinctive three-part close harmonies rehearsed since childhood. Robin's vibrato lead was the hallmark of their earlier hits such as 'Massachusetts' (1968). In their second phase of major success, prompted after they wrote and sang the soundtrack for the film *Saturday Night Fever* – the biggest-selling soundtrack of all time – it was Barry's falsetto that defined their sound. At least 2500 artists have recorded their songs. There are more than 400 versions of 'How Deep Is Your Love'.

In 2004 Barry and Robin were appointed a CBE and their nephew Adam collected the honour on behalf of his father, Maurice, who had died suddenly in 2003. Robin died after a battle with cancer in 2012. In 2013 Barry went on tour, keeping the group's name alive with his son Steve and Maurice's daughter Samantha.

QUEEN

JOHN DEACON
BRIAN MAY
FREDDIE MERCURY
ROGER TAYLOR

Queen have been responsible for writing some of the most brilliantly conceived and executed songs and arrangements in popular music. Early hits such as 'Killer Queen' and 'Bohemian Rhapsody' revealed new depths of sophistication and ingenuity. While much attention naturally focused on charismatic lead singer Freddie Mercury, their musical achievements were clearly a joint effort, with all four members contributing hit singles to the band's catalogue in a dazzling variety of styles. Mercury's diversity included 'Somebody To Love' and 'Crazy Little Thing Called Love'; Brian May's unique guitar sound drove his songs such as 'Hammer To Fall' and 'We Will Rock You'; bass player John Deacon penned 'I Want To Break Free' and 'Another One Bites The Dust' (one of the band's biggest hits in the US) and drummer Roger Taylor wrote hits including 'Radio Ga Ga' and 'A Kind Of Magic'. Early albums from the debut *Queen* (1973) displayed hard rock roots but diversified into a wider range of styles on *Sheer Heart Attack* (1974) and *A Night At The Opera* (1975), which yielded 'Bohemian Rhapsody'. Further hits 'We Will Rock You' and 'We Are The Champions' made them stadium rock heroes, a role that was sealed with their 'Live Aid' performance of 1985. Freddie died of bronchopneumonia brought on by AIDS in 1991 and an all-star tribute concert at Wembley Stadium drew 72,000 fans. Having sold 300 million albums, Queen received a special BPI Award in 1990, were inducted into the Rock and Roll Hall of Fame in 2001 and inducted into the Songwriters Hall of Fame on June 12, 2003. Queen were recognised for their million selling achievements over three decades by the Songwriters Hall of Fame and in particular for the distinction of being the only group in which each of its members have achieved No. 1 songs.

DAVID BOWIE

In 2013 Bowie announced the release of his first album in a decade, after having reportedly retired. *The Next Day* hit No. 1 on iTunes in 40 countries from Armenia to Vietnam. It was a surprising but typical move by the 66-year-old singer/songwriter who had been creating waves since the Sixties. Born David Robert Jones in Brixton, London (January 8, 1947), he grew up in Bromley, Kent, where he formed the Konrads in 1962. By 1966 he had changed his surname to Bowie. The original songs on his debut album *David Bowie* (1967) had a theatrical feel, as did the smash hit single 'Space Oddity' (1969). Bowie then morphed from smart Mod to androgynous rocker with *The Man Who Sold The World* (1970). Subsequent albums *Hunky Dory* (1971) and *The Rise And Fall Of Ziggy Stardust And The Spiders From Mars* (1972) won Bowie international fame along with a string of hit singles, lavish touring productions and acting roles in films and on stage. As an artist and composer, it could be said he remains in a permanent state of evolution.

STOCK, AITKEN & WATERMAN

MIKE STOCK
MATT AITKEN
PETE WATERMAN, OBE

Mike Stock, Matt Aitken and Pete Waterman dominated the world's charts in the late Eighties and Nineties. In their heyday, the trio scored 100 Top 40 hits and sold 40 million records in the UK alone, making them one of the most successful songwriting and production partnerships of all time.

SAW are best remembered for their trademark Hi-NRG-inflected pop, but their catalogue reveals diverse contemporary influences, with Princess's 'Say I'm Your Number One' widely considered a bona fide classic of UK soul. Motown was also a key template not only for SAW's songwriting but also Waterman's PWL 'Hit Factory' – the London studio complex, production company and eventual record label at which they were based.

SAW launched a host of new artists with pop anthems such as Mel & Kim's 'Respectable', Rick Astley's 'Never Gonna Give You Up' and Kylie Minogue's 'I Should Be So Lucky', but proved equally adept at penning major hits for established acts, with Bananarama's 'Love In The First Degree' becoming their best-selling single and 'This Time I Know It's For Real' the biggest post-Seventies success for original disco queen Donna Summer.

Aitken left the partnership in 1991, followed by Stock two years later. Many SAW-produced acts reunited at Hit Factory Live, a one-off show at the O$_2$ in 2012.

SIR ELTON JOHN CBE & BERNIE TAUPIN

T he legendary partnership of Sir Elton John and Bernie Taupin began in 1967 after both answered a 'talent wanted' ad in a music paper.

Sir Elton (born Reginald Kenneth Dwight in Pinner, Middlesex, March 25, 1947), a pianist from age three, began playing in bands in the Sixties. He went on to sell more than 250 million records after developing an unusual method of working with Taupin.

Taupin (born Lincolnshire, May 22, 1950) had a love of literature, nature and the arts instilled by his mother and grandfather. His first lyrics for John were put in the post and ever since the music has been fitted to the words, contrary to most songwriting duos. The album *Elton John* (1970) featuring 'Your Song' established their international reputation. Between 1970 and 1976, 14 albums were recorded including the classic *Goodbye Yellow Brick Road*.

Countless awards and achievements include composing the biggest-selling single of all time 'Candle In The Wind 1997', a re-worked version of an earlier hit which became their tribute to the late Princess of Wales. The cover of the 2006 album *The Captain And The Kid* shows both writers together for the first time, marking 40 years of their partnership.

Taupin moved to California in the mid-Seventies where he now has a ranch, fulfilling a lifetime dream. Sir Elton, who gave a concert on his 60th birthday in New York, began a three-year run at Caesar's Palace, Las Vegas, in 2011.

MARC BOLAN

Marc Bolan was the glam rock star of the Seventies who reinvented himself after first bopping onto the music scene in the Sixties. With his good looks and distinctive vocal style backed by the bongo drums of Steve Peregrin Took, he appealed to festival-going hippies. Shortening his band's name from Tyrannosaurus Rex to T. Rex, his wizardry with words and catchy themes caught the attention of record buyers. In 1970 he electrified his signature rolling back-beat and glammed up with feathers and glitter to record 'Ride A White Swan'. That hit was followed by more charting singles 'Hot Love' and 'Get It On', which spent four weeks at No. 1. Other classic T. Rex hits were 'Telegram Sam' and 'Metal Guru'. Marc (born Mark Feld, Stoke Newington, London, September 30, 1947) died in a car crash on September 16, 1977 just as he was staging a UK comeback. In 2012, the 35th anniversary of his death was marked by the *PRS for Music* Members Benevolent Fund with a tribute concert in London.

ROD TEMPERTON

W ho would guess that a guy from Cleetho[...]
Thriller, the biggest selling album of a[...]
[T]emperton (born October 15, 1947) woke one o[...]
He wrote three songs on Michael Jackson's *Off[...]
[th]ree for *Thriller*.

At school in Lincolnshire he had started out[...]
[d]rummer, going on to keyboards. He joined the[...]
[fu]nk/disco band Heatwave in 1975. Soon his o[...]
[b]eing heard and 'Boogie Nights' and the ballad[...]
[t]he album *Too Hot To Handle* were hits in the U[...]
[1]978 he left the band to concentrate on writing[...]
[t]o write for Jackson resulting in 'Rock With Yo[...]
[']Off The Wall' (1979). He also wrote 'Baby Be [...]
[a]nd the title track for *Thriller* (1982), the Gram[...]
[th]at had enormous worldwide impact, enhance[...]
[T]hriller video that elevated Michael Jackson to[...]

As a prolific composer and producer, Rod ha[...]
[A]merica, working with both pop and jazz artist[...]
[El]la Fitzgerald, George Benson and Herbie Ha[...]

He was nominated for an Oscar as co-writer o[...]
[1]985 film *The Color Purple*.

[Ph]otograph by Lucy Sewill, Soho Studios, London, Decembe[r ...]

JEFF LYNNE

Jeff Lynne, leader of the Electric Light Orchestra, which reached its zenith in 1979 with the multi-million selling album *Discovery*, was also co-founder of the Traveling Wilburys.

Born in Birmingham (December 30, 1947), the multi-instrumentalist, composer, songwriter, arranger and record producer learned production methods on a reel-to-reel tape recorder before joining The Move in 1970 and then leading the Electric Light Orchestra. ELO's first album won fans with its fusion of rock and classical music. Later hit albums include *Out Of The Blue* (1977).

The 1980 film *Xanadu* featured ELO numbers and was adapted as a Broadway musical. After *Time* topped the album charts in 1980, Lynne turned to producing. In 1988 he joined Tom Petty, Bob Dylan, Roy Orbison and George Harrison to form the Traveling Wilburys. In 1990 he released his first solo album and worked with the surviving Beatles on the 1994 *Anthology* album. More recently Lynne released his first solo record in 20 years, *Long Wave*, and the masterfully re-recorded *Mr. Blue Sky: The Very Best Of Electric Light Orchestra*, which both debuted in the UK Top 10 in the same week of 2012. Lynne has received three Ivor Novello Awards for Outstanding Contributions to British Music.

EDDY GRANT

Ringbang

S ince his song 'Baby Come Back' was a No. 1 hit for The Equals (1968), and their final hit together 'Black Skin Blue-Eyed Boys' (1970), Eddy Grant has made an impact on the music industry with his cross-genre pop songs, some with overtly political lyrics, such as his first solo hit single 'Living On The Frontline' (1979).

Born in Plaisance Village, Guyana (March 5, 1948), Edmond Montague Grant moved to Kentish Town, London, where he attended Acland Burghley school. He played trumpet in the school's orchestra and eventually made his first guitar under the guidance of his woodwork master. In 1969 he established his first publishing company, Grant Music Limited, and his first record label, Torpedo Records.

He established Europe's first black-owned professional recording studio (Coach House, 1974) and ultimately the first black-owned record manufacturing plant in Europe (the British Homophone Record Manufacturing Plant, 1979).

His 1982 solo single 'I Don't Wanna Dance' spent three weeks at No. 1 in the UK, and did the same in almost every other territory. The same year his *Killer On The Rampage* album made the Top 10 in a similar manner. The following year 'Electric Avenue' hit the No. 2 chart position on both sides of the Atlantic, becoming another of Grant's many multi-million sellers worldwide.

In 1981 Grant moved to Barbados where his Bluewave Recording Studio has played host to many of the world's most famous recording artists and songwriters, while his companies Ice Records and Ice Music Limited own and control the most prestigious classic calypso recordings and song copyrights in the world.

In 1988, Eddy achieved a Top 10 hit with 'Gimme Hope Jo'anna', which is without doubt the most popular anti-apartheid anthem, and was banned in South Africa by the government of the time. In the early Nineties, Eddy applied the name 'Ringbang' to a Caribbean music genre and philosophy of his own invention.

Legend has it that no other artist/songwriter has retained greater ownership and control over his entire catalogue of works than Eddy Grant has over a career of almost 50 years to date.

ANDREW LLOYD WEBBER

Andrew Lloyd Webber (born London, March 22, 1948) has made an enormous contribution to music and theatre, both as a composer and as a producer, bringing a string of hit musical shows and memorable songs to the world stage. He began writing music at the age of nine and staged productions in a self-built toy theatre. He went to Westminster School and studied history briefly at Magdalen College, Oxford but left to work with lyricist Tim Rice.

Lloyd Webber's shows include *Joseph And The Amazing Technicolor Dreamcoat* (1968), *Jesus Christ Superstar* (1970), *Evita* (1978) and *Cats* (1981, which ran in London for 21 years and on Broadway for 18 years), *Starlight Express* (1984), *The Phantom Of The Opera* (1986, which celebrated its 25th anniversary in the West End in 2012 and is the longest running show in the history of Broadway), *Aspects Of Love* (1989), *Sunset Boulevard* (1993), *Whistle Down The Wind* (1998), *The Beautiful Game* (2000), *The Woman In White* (2004), *Love Never Dies* (2010) and *Stephen Ward* (2013). His best-known songs include 'Memory', 'Don't Cry For Me Argentina', 'The Music Of The Night', 'I Don't Know How To Love Him', 'No Matter What', 'Love Changes Everything' and 'Pie Jesu'. Lloyd Webber has also composed two film scores and a Latin Requiem Mass.

He was knighted in 1992 and made an honorary life peer in 1997 for his services to music. Copious awards include seven Tony Awards, three Grammys, an Academy Award, 14 Ivor Novello Awards, seven Olivier Awards, a Golden Globe and a Kennedy Center Honor. He has been hailed as one of the most successful composers in history.

Photograph by Lucy Sewill, London, February 27, 2014.

BRIAN ENO

Influential musician, composer, record producer and visual artist Brian Eno has made an indelible contribution to musical culture in a career which has spanned mainstream rock and the outer limits of the avant-garde. He is credited with pioneering the genre of ambient music, as well as establishing important creative relationships with many other artists, notably Robert Fripp, David Byrne and David Bowie, and the bands Roxy Music, U2 and Coldplay. His influence can be felt in a broad range of cultural contexts from the familiar 'start-up' tone used on Microsoft's Windows 95 software through to the spectrum of modern electronic music.

Born in Woodbridge, Suffolk (May 15, 1948), Eno studied art at Winchester College, where he shared the same teachers as Pete Townshend, who became an early influence. He began using a tape recorder as a musical instrument in experimental bands, and joined Roxy Music in 1971. He left the band in 1973 after their *For Your Pleasure* album, he embarked on a solo career, releasing the critically acclaimed albums *Here Come The Warm Jets, Taking Tiger Mountain (By Strategy)* – featuring the driving rocker 'Third Uncle' – *Another Green World* and *Before And After Science*.

Eno also worked with King Crimson guitarist Robert Fripp on *(No Pussyfooting)* (1973) using a tape delay system they called Frippertronics. He also produced albums by the Portsmouth Sinfonia and many ambient electronic and acoustic albums, including the classic *Ambient 1: Music For Airports* and *Music For Films* (both 1978).

He has also scored music for films such as Peter Jackson's *The Lovely Bones* and won a BAFTA for his music for Channel 4's *Top Boy* in 2012.

Proliferating projects as one of music's most revered producers include working with David Bowie on the 'Berlin Trilogy' of albums (1977–79) and production roles with Talking Heads, Devo, Ultravox and James. He won Best Producer Award at the 1994 and 1996 Brit Awards. A long-running relationship with U2 began with *The Unforgettable Fire* (1984) and Eno has contributed to several key albums by the Irish band since, writing with the band on *No Line On The Horizon* (2009). He also produced Coldplay's album *Viva La Vida or Death And All His Friends* (2008), and produced and co-wrote *Mylo Xyloto* (2011).

YUSUF/CAT STEVENS

Yusuf Islam (born Steven Demetre Georgiou, London, July 21, 1948) was known as Cat Stevens during the early Seventies when his classic folk rock albums *Tea For The Tillerman* and *Teaser And The Firecat* catapulted him to international success as a singer/songwriter.

He converted to Islam in 1977 after a life-threatening illness prompted an epiphany which robbed millions of fans of seeing how his music would have developed. For decades he devoted himself to philanthropic and educational Muslim causes, but returned to making music as Yusuf in 2006 with *An Other Cup*, his first album for 28 years.

The son of a Greek-Cypriot father and Swedish mother, he grew up above a London restaurant run by his parents. Up on the roof, while learning to play the guitar, he breathed in inspiration from the sounds wafting from nearby Denmark Street. He began playing his songs in cafes and pubs, choosing his stage name in part because a girlfriend said he had eyes like a cat, but mainly because of his doubts over whether anyone would go to a record shop and ask for 'that Steven Demetre Georgiou album'.

Yusuf released his latest album *Roadsinger* in 2009, and in May 2014 was inducted into the Rock and Roll Hall of Fame.

FRANCIS ROSSI OBE
& RICK PARFITT OBE

As founder members of one of the UK's much loved bands, Status Quo, Rossi and Parfitt formed an enduring musical performing partnership. Rossi (guitar and vocals) was born in Forest Green, London (May 29, 1949). His first group was called the Spectres which formed in 1962. They changed the name to Status Quo when Rick Parfitt (guitar and vocals) joined in 1967. Parfitt, born in Woking, Surrey (October 12, 1948), was playing with cabaret group The Highlights at a Butlins holiday camp when he first met Rossi. The revamped group's first hit was with Rossi's composition 'Pictures Of Matchstick Men' a UK No. 7 hit in 1968. A change of image engaged Quo with hard rock audiences and in 1972 they scored a UK Top 10 hit with 'Paper Plane'. Their Seventies hits included 'Caroline' and 'Down Down' composed by Rossi with Bob Young, and 'Whatever You Want' by Parfitt with keyboard player Andy Bown. After a break in the early Eighties, Quo returned with 'Marguerita Time' (1983) and 'In The Army Now' (1986). Rick and Francis both received OBEs in 2010.

MIKE BATT LVO

Mike Batt, composer, arranger, producer and conductor, is known to millions for his creation of the Wombles group, following the success of the children's TV series of the Seventies, and many hits including 'Bright Eyes' for Art Garfunkel.

Born in Southampton (February 6, 1949), Batt signed, at the age of 18, as songwriter and artist to Liberty/United Artists Records, soon becoming head of A&R. His later Womble songs and productions resulted in eight hit singles and four gold albums. His solo albums as a singer include *Tarot Suite* with the London Symphony Orchestra. He composed and produced the four million-selling album *The Violin Player* that launched classical violinist Vanessa-Mae.

Many of his compositions have been used to mark historic events, including the official anthem for the opening of the Channel Tunnel. Forming Dramatico Records in 2002, he discovered Katie Melua, writing many of her songs including 'The Closest Thing To Crazy' and 'Nine Million Bicycles', and selling 11 million albums. He is deputy chairman of the BPI and has served on the boards of many industry organisations including BASCA and the Performing Right Society. In 2013 he was made Lieutenant of the Royal Victoria Order for services to the Royal Household.

Batt is a five times Ivor Novello Award winner.

Photograph by Lucy Sewill, at Mike Batt's home, January 7, 2014.

TREVOR HORN CBE

Groundbreaking record producer and songwriter Trevor Horn is also a first-class musician and singer who has charted as a performer with three bands. Trevor (born in Durham, July 15, 1949) became a session musician in the Seventies playing bass, guitar and keyboards and building a home studio. He formed The Buggles with Geoff Downes and co-wrote their 1979 hit 'Video Killed The Radio Star'. He joined prog rockers Yes in 1979 and later produced their successful 1983 comeback album *90125*.

Horn also founded pioneering concept outfit Art of Noise but one of his major successes was producing hit records for Frankie Goes to Hollywood in the Eighties. Horn has three Brit Awards and a Grammy (1996) for producing Seal's 'Kiss From A Rose'. A 2004 Wembley Arena concert marked his 25 years as a record producer and resulted in the double album *Produced By Trevor Horn*. Horn has written for TV and films, and produced *Reality Killed The Video Star* for Robbie Williams (2009). He was appointed a CBE in 2011.

Photograph by Lucy Sewill, Sarm Studios, London, January 14, 2014.

MARK KNOPFLER OBE

A master guitarist, a distinctive singer, composer and record producer, Mark Knopfler has been a stimulating force since first emerging as a co-founder of Dire Straits in 1977. Much sought after by fellow artists, he has recorded and performed with Bob Dylan, Van Morrison, Randy Newman, Eric Clapton and the late Chet Atkins. Born in Glasgow and growing up in Newcastle upon Tyne, he became a journalist in Leeds on leaving school and worked as a teacher for three years after graduating from Leeds University. While sharing a flat in Deptford, South London, with his guitarist brother David, they began playing Mark's early compositions. A demo tape landed a contract with Vertigo and the *Dire Straits* album released in June 1978 topped charts around the world accompanied by the hit single 'Sultans Of Swing'. There followed an extraordinary leap to international success capped by the award-winning *Brothers In Arms* (1985) and the hit single 'Money For Nothing'. Knopfler has also recorded several solo albums, composed film scores and is the recipient of a host of awards including four Grammys and an OBE.

Photograph by Lucy Sewill, British Grove Studios, London, January 22, 2014.

PETER GABRIEL

The multi-faceted career of Peter Gabriel (born in Chobham, Surrey, February 13, 1950) began with Genesis in 1967, where as lead singer and flautist he contributed to the success of such groundbreaking concept albums as *Trespass*, *Foxtrot* and the epic *The Lamb Lies Down On Broadway*. Having pioneered the use of flamboyant costumes and special effects on stage, he left Genesis in 1975 to launch a solo career, releasing four eponymously titled albums. Gabriel's debut solo single 'Solsbury Hill' was a Top 20 hit single in 1977.

His 1980 UK No. 1 album *So* yielded three Top 20 singles among them his duet with Kate Bush 'Don't Give Up' and 'Sledgehammer' accompanied by an award-winning video. Gabriel has received 13 MTV awards, three Brits, six Grammys and the first Pioneer Award at the BT Digital Music Awards. He received a Man of Peace Award from the Nobel Peace Prize Laureates in 2006. He was inducted into the Rock and Roll Hall of Fame in April 2014.

JOAN ARMATRADING MBE

Lyrics that probe the anguish and pain of love sung with an appropriately deep, rich voice ensured Joan Armatrading the distinction of being the first British female singer/songwriter to enjoy international success.

Born on the Caribbean island of Saint Kitts (December 9, 1950), she moved to Brookfields, Birmingham, aged seven. In her teens she taught herself guitar on a £3 instrument, later getting fired from her first job for playing during tea breaks. She linked up with lyricist Pam Nestor for her debut album and their only collaboration, *Whatever's For Us* (1972). Appearances on John Peel's radio show in the Seventies raised her profile. Her 1976 hit single 'Love And Affection' was jazz influenced but by 1980 her style became harder and more pop oriented ('Me Myself I').

In 2007 Joan became the first UK female artist to debut at No. 1 in the Billboard Blues Chart. Her honours include an Ivor Novello Award (1996) and honorary degrees from the Royal Scottish Academy of Music and Drama, the University of the West Indies and five other universities including the Open University from which she gained a BA (Hons) degree in History in 2001. She was made MBE the same year.

Photograph by Lucy Sewill, The Rathbone Hotel, London, December 6, 2013.

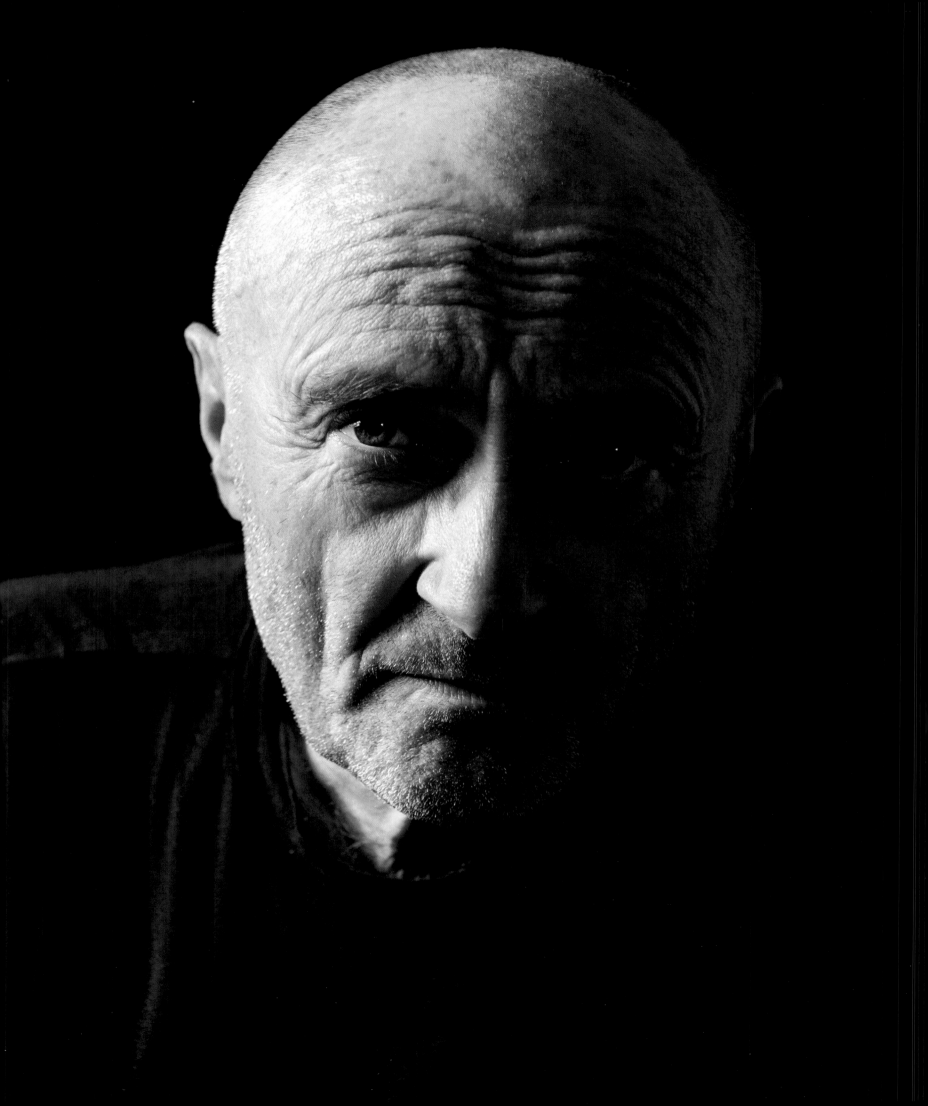

PHIL COLLINS LVO

A multi-instrumentalist, songwriter, actor and writer, Phil Collins also has an honorary degree from a Texas university for his research into the Alamo.

Quoted as only setting out to 'earn a living as a drummer', instead he drew worldwide acclaim with a career launched when he answered a *Melody Maker* advert for a 'drummer sensitive to acoustic music' placed by Genesis. For the next five years he contributed his signature big drum sound to the globally successful band, moving into the lead vocalist slot in 1975 when Peter Gabriel left.

Born in Hounslow, Middlesex (January 30, 1951), Collins developed his solo career alongside Genesis in the Eighties, finally leaving the band in 1996. The album *We Can't Dance* was his last as lead singer. His debut solo album *Face Value* (1981) topped the charts in seven countries. He has sold 150 million records worldwide as a solo artist, his most successful album being *No Jacket Required*.

His industry prizes include seven Grammy and six Brit Awards, while a string of US awards include induction into the Rock and Roll Hall of Fame. Collins has also won an Oscar for best song for 'You'll Be In My Heart' from *Tarzan* (1999). As a producer he has worked with Adam Ant, Philip Bailey, John Martyn, Frida Lyngstad and Eric Clapton. He acted the lead role in the 1988 film *Buster* and was appointed Lieutenant of the Royal Victorian Order for his work for the Prince's Trust in 1994.

In 2013 he announced his return to songwriting after retiring in 2006.

Photograph by Lucy Sewill, The Dorchester Hotel, London, February 6, 2014

STING (GORDON SUMNER, CBE)

Sting is now known as much for his championing of social and political causes as for his singing and songwriting. *Time* magazine in 2011 named him one of the 100 most influential people in the world.

Born Gordon Sumner (Northumberland, October 2, 1951), his nickname turned stage name originated from the striped bee-like sweater he wore while playing bass in jazz bands. He gave up a teaching job before moving to London in 1977 and forming The Police. During the next decade, the band produced five chart-topping albums. Their last album, *Synchronicity*, included their most successful single 'Every Breath You Take'. The group had sold 50 million albums before disbanding in 1986. They later reformed for a 2007–2008 world tour, playing to over 3.7 million people on five continents.

As a solo artist, Sting has enjoyed several hits, notably 'Fields Of Gold' from his 1993 album *Ten Summoner's Tales*. His first musical, *The Last Ship*, inspired by his memories of the seafaring town of Wallsend in the north of England where he was born and raised, premiered in Chicago in June 2014 before its Broadway debut in the fall. His numerous accolades include 16 Grammys, an Emmy and three Oscar nominations for Best Original Song.

BOB GELDOF KBE & MIDGE URE OBE

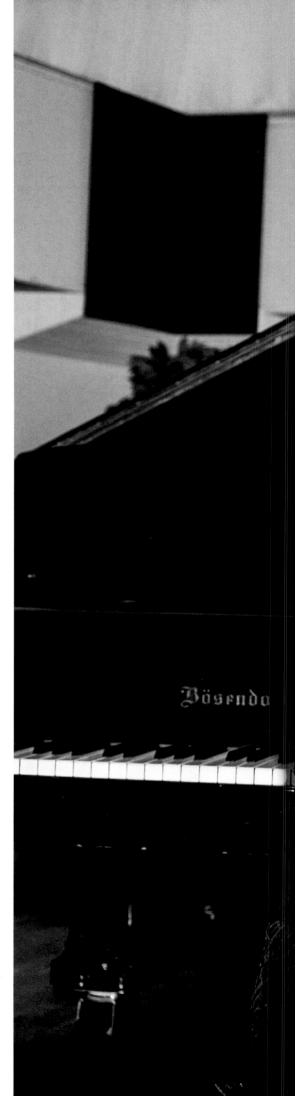

Bob Geldof and Midge Ure each enjoy varied and successful musical careers and together boosted the world's attitude to charity fund raising by giving the concept attitude. Geldof's colourful language during their 'Live Aid' concert in 1985 raised the giving rate to £300 per second. In all, £150 million was raised.

James Ure (born in Lanarkshire, Scotland, October 10, 1953), a singer/songwriter, guitarist and keyboard player, had success in the Seventies and Eighties with Slik, Thin Lizzy, Rich Kids and Visage until becoming frontman of synth rock band Ultravox in 1979. Their fourth album *Vienna* (1980) marked a change of style and took them into the charts. Ure is also a record producer and as a solo artist his successes include the No. 1 single 'If I Was'. Ultravox reformed in 2009.

Robert Frederick Zenon Geldof (born in County Dublin, Eire, October 5, 1951) had ten hits and platinum albums in the Seventies and Eighties with the Boomtown Rats, the first Irish group to have a UK No. 1 with 'Rat Trap'. The Rats also reunited, after a 26-year hiatus, for the 2013 Isle of Wight Festival. Geldof and Ure interrupted their solo activities to co-write 'Do They Know It's Christmas?' in 1984, the fastest-selling single in UK history, which raised £8 million for famine relief. They went on to raise billions with the Band Aid, Live Aid and Live 8 globally televised events – the biggest in history. Midge Ure is an ambassador for Save the Children and Geldof's humanitarian activities include working for debt relief, third world trade and AIDS relief in Africa.

Midge Ure was made OBE in 2005 for his services to music and charity and Bob Geldof received an honorary knighthood, aged 34, in 1986.

Photograph by Lucy Sewill, Sarm Studios (formerly known as Sarm West Studios), London, January 14, 2014. This was the studio used for the original recording of the Band Aid single, 'Do They Know It's Christmas?' in November 1984. Bob Geldof and Midge Ure were last photographed together there almost 30 years ago. This is the first picture taken of them together at Sarm since.

IRON MAIDEN

BRUCE DICKINSON
JANICK GERS
STEVE HARRIS
NICKO McBRAIN
DAVE MURRAY
ADRIAN SMITH

Iron Maiden are one of rock's most successful and internationally popular bands. Armed with a plethora of hit albums and singles, the group, founded by bass player and chief songwriter Steve Harris in London in 1975, has gained critical respect and a fanatically loyal worldwide following.

A blend of skilful musicianship and composing expertise elevates Maiden's work to a high level, while retaining metal's basic requirement to shock and awe. Named after a medieval instrument of torture, Maiden played their first shows at a pub in Stratford in 1976 and very quickly garnered a devoted fan base who identified with the band's memorable songs, raw onstage energy and sheer musical power. In 1979 manager Rod Smallwood saw them signed to EMI and their debut album *Iron Maiden* (1980) began the trajectory that was fully realised by 1982's *The Number Of The Beast*. This was the first album to feature vocalist Bruce Dickinson and catapulted them from UK to international stardom. Throughout the decades that followed, Maiden recorded and toured relentlessly, cementing their reputation as one of the hardest-working bands on the planet and always accompanied by their iconic band mascot Eddie, who adorns every album cover and T-shirt and makes an onstage appearance at all their live shows.

Their 15th and most recent studio album, *The Final Frontier* (2010), shot to No. 1 in 28 countries, becoming their biggest chart success to date. This was accompanied by a 98-date world tour playing to over two million fans utilising their specially customized Boeing 757 airliner Ed Force One piloted by Bruce Dickinson. The plane transported band, crew and their entire 10 ton stage production 50,000 miles right around the globe, allowing Maiden to continue their trail-blazing reputation for taking metal to new frontiers. Having first played in Poland and behind the Iron Curtain in 1984 at the height of the Cold War, the band also toured throughout South America, initially in 1992 and many times since, including a show at Chile's Estadio Nacional in 2013 to over 60,000 fans, which was the largest audience ever in Chile for a British band. With visits to the Middle East and India in 2007 and Indonesia in 2011, the desire to seek out new places to play allows the band to reach an even wider audience and thus their legacy continues to grow as new generations of fans join the Maiden 'family'.

Included in the many and varied accolades throughout Maiden's career are a Grammy Award for Best Metal Performance for album track 'El Dorado' (2011), an Ivor Novello International Achievement Award (2002) and Best British Live Act BRIT Award (2009).

In 2012–2014 the band embarked on its Maiden England World Tour, climaxing three decades of achievement. Despite lack of TV or radio support, the band have sold over 90 million albums and played over 2000 concerts in 59 countries. They are still recording and touring and are one of the few bands to have not only remained contemporary over time but also increased in popularity and relevance.

THE CLASH

JOE STRUMMER
MICK JONES
PAUL SIMONON

Pioneering punk rockers The Clash (1976–1986) were fronted by lead vocalist and rhythm guitarist Joe Strummer. The other members were Mick Jones (lead guitar and vocals), Paul Simonon (bass guitar and vocals) and Nicky 'Topper' Headon (drums). Their eponymous debut album in 1977 gained attention with its rebellious, political lyrics and aggressive sound. Fame spread to the US with the release of third album *London Calling*, while 'Rock The Casbah', from later album *Combat Rock*, propelled them into the US Top 10. After internal disputes, The Clash carried on with a new line-up until finally disbanding in 1986.

Joe Strummer (born in Turkey, August 21, 1952) died at his Somerset home on December 22, 2002. A mural tribute to the musician was unveiled in New York in 2013.

In 2003 the band, including original drummer Terry Chimes, were inducted into the Rock and Roll Hall of Fame.

DAVE STEWART & ANNIE LENNOX OBE

Dave Stewart (born in Sunderland, September 9, 1952) and Annie Lennox (born in Aberdeen, December 25, 1954) first met in a London restaurant in 1975.

With shared tastes in music, they formed a band called The Tourists together with fellow songwriter Peet Coombes, going on to record three albums and touring extensively for several years. The Tourists disbanded in 1979 when Dave and Annie decided to take a different route.

Experimenting with synthesisers and electronic music, they created a unique style of memorably crafted songs under the title of Eurythmics. In 1983, their second album, *Sweet Dreams (Are Made of This)*, was released, with the title track becoming a worldwide hit, topping the charts in various countries including the US, where they were at the cutting edge of the MTV generation. The duo went on to release a string of hit singles and albums before they parted company in 1990.

In 1992 Annie released her highly successful debut album *Diva*, while Dave embarked on a parallel music career, writing film scripts and musicals, releasing solo albums and working as a sought-after record producer, collaborating with the likes of U2, Mick Jagger, Bryan Ferry and a plethora of internationally acclaimed artists.

Eurythmics have won a number of awards, including an MTV Video Music Award for Best New Artist in 1984, the Grammy Award for Best Rock Performance by a Duo or Group with Vocal in 1987, two Ivor Novello Awards for Songwriters of the Year in 1984 and 1987, the Brit Award for Outstanding Contribution to Music in 1999, the Silver Clef Award for Outstanding Contribution to UK Music in 2000, and in 2005 they were inducted into the UK Music Hall of Fame. Eurythmics have sold an estimated 80 million albums.

PATRICK DOYLE

Multi-award-winning composer Patrick Doyle has worked with some of the most acclaimed directors in the world, including Alfonso Cuarón, Régis Wargnier, Brian De Palma, Ang Lee, Mike Newell and Robert Altman. His filmography includes *Sense And Sensibility* (1995), *Gosford Park* (2001), *Harry Potter And The Goblet Of Fire* (2005), *Rise Of The Planet Of The Apes* (2011) and *Brave* (2012).

Born in Lanarkshire (April 6, 1953), Doyle graduated from the Royal Scottish Academy of Music and joined the Renaissance Theatre Company in 1987, established by Kenneth Branagh and David Parfitt. In 1989, his hymn 'Non Nobis Domine' from Branagh's acclaimed *Henry V* was awarded the Ivor Novello Award for Best Film Theme. Doyle has subsequently collaborated with Branagh on 11 feature films, including *Dead Again* (1991), *Thor* (2011), *Jack Ryan: Shadow Recruit* (2014) and the forthcoming *Cinderella* (2015).

Doyle has been nominated for two Academy Awards, two César Awards and two Golden Globes. He has received a Lifetime Achievement Award from Scottish BAFTA, the Henry Mancini Award from ASCAP and the PRS Award for Extraordinary Achievement in Music.

In 1997, Doyle was diagnosed with leukemia, from which he made a full recovery. The following year, Branagh directed his 'Music From The Movies' concert at the Royal Albert Hall in aid of Leukemia Research, which starred Dame Judi Dench, Emma Thompson and Alan Rickman, among many others. In 2013, the London Symphony Orchestra honoured Doyle with a special concert for his 60th birthday at the Barbican. The sell-out performance featured some of his best-loved scores, and stars performing included Emma Thompson and Sir Derek Jacobi.

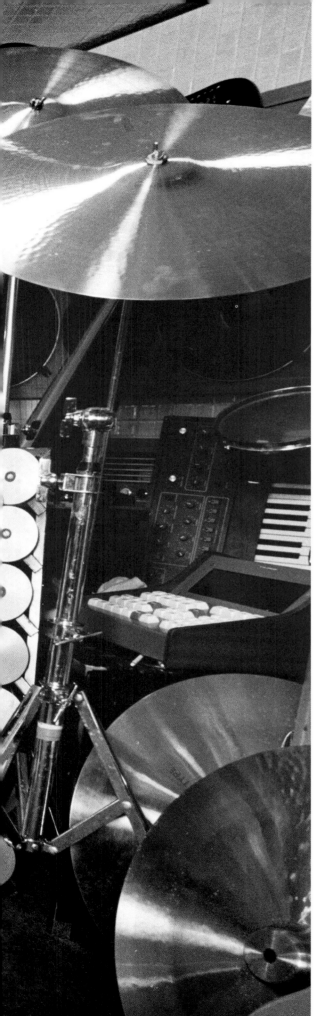

MIKE OLDFIELD

Mike Oldfield is best known as the composer and performer of *Tubular Bells*, the instrumental album that launched Virgin Records. Oldfield (born in Reading, May 15, 1953) played more than 20 instruments on the multi-layered recording, which was later used on the soundtrack of *The Exorcist*.

His unusual guitar style, using fingers and nails to produce vibrato effects, was honed as a teenager while playing folk clubs. After the success of *Tubular Bells*, Oldfield released *Hergest Ridge* in 1974. Many of his albums were produced at his home studios using an array of synthesisers and keyboards. They include *Tubular Bells II* (1992) and *Tubular Bells III* (1998), *The Millennium Bell* (1999) and *Tubular Bells 2003*. His other works include albums *Ommadawn* (1975) and *Incantations* (1978). His first classical album *Music Of The Spheres* topped the UK classical chart in 2008. In 2012 he performed *Tubular Bells* at the London Olympic Games opening ceremony. His latest album, *Man On The Rocks,* was released in March 2014.

JUDITH WEIR CBE

The prolific composer Judith Weir (born in Cambridge, May 11, 1954) draws inspiration from the music and legends of many different cultures. *Natural History* is a setting of four Taoist texts for soprano and orchestra, while *King Harald's Saga* is perhaps the world's most compressed historical epic. Her first major opera, commissioned by the BBC, *A Night At The Chinese Opera*, was praised for its fusion of Eastern and Western styles. She has written concert works for several notable singers including Jessye Norman.

Weir trained with John Tavener while at school before studying at King's College, Cambridge. The traditions of Scotland, reflecting her parentage, are also evident in her work. She has worked in India with storyteller Vayu Naidu and on film and music collaborations with director Margaret Williams. Her awards include the Lincoln Center's Stoeger Prize (1997), the 2001 *South Bank Show* Music Award and the Queen's Medal for Music in 2007. She was made CBE in 1995.

PET SHOP BOYS

NEIL TENNANT
CHRIS LOWE

Masters of electronic pop music, Neil Tennant (born July 10, 1954) and Chris Lowe (born October 4, 1959) created a powerful diversion from mainstream rock during the Eighties. Hailed as the UK's most successful pop duo, they have sold more than 50 million records around the world since 1982. 'West End Girls', 'It's A Sin' and 'Always On My Mind' are among their tally of 42 UK Top 30 singles and 22 Top 10 hits. Tennant and Lowe met in a Chelsea shop in 1981. Discovering a mutual interest in dance music, they began writing songs together. The name Pet Shop Boys came from a local pet shop where a friend worked. Visiting New York, Tennant met producer Bobby Orlando and played him a demo tape. Orlando went on to record many of the Pet Shop Boys' early tracks including 'West End Girls', a US club favourite in 1984. The duo signed to Parlophone and re-recorded 'West End Girls'. A No. 1 around the world, it sold 1.5 million copies. Much in demand, the Pet Shop Boys have worked with a variety of artists including Dusty Springfield, David Bowie and Madonna.

CHRIS DIFFORD & GLENN TILBROOK OF SQUEEZE

Narrative tales told with tongue-twisting delivery and dark humour were the forte of Squeeze, epitomised by seminal hit 'Up The Junction'. The group's clever songs were written by lyricist Chris Difford (guitar and vocals) and composer Glenn Tilbrook (guitar and vocals). Formed in Deptford, South London in 1974, Squeeze also originally included Jools Holland on keyboards. The 1978 debut album *Squeeze* (A&M) produced by John Cale yielded the dramatic 'Take Me I'm Yours' notable for elaborate lyrics and insistent rock riffs. Chris and Glenn were critically acclaimed as songwriters when further hits followed with 'Black Coffee In Bed' and 'Another Nail In My Heart'. The second album *Cool For Cats* (1979) yielded the title track and 'Up The Junction', both Top 5 hits. Squeeze broke up in 1982 but reformed in 1985 and again in 2007. The group's early days in South London were commemorated with a Heritage Award from *PRS for Music* in 2010. Squeeze have continued to tour and record into 2014.

Photograph by Lucy Sewill, 45RPM, London, January 28, 2014.

JOY DIVISION

IAN CURTIS
PETER HOOK
STEPHEN MORRIS
BERNARD SUMNER

Pioneers of the Seventies post-punk movement, Joy Division shot to fame with the debut album *Unknown Pleasures* and hit single 'Love Will Tear Us Apart'. The group formed in Salford, Manchester in 1976 and was fronted by singer Ian Curtis together with Bernard Sumner (guitar, keyboards), Peter Hook (bass) and Stephen Morris (drums). Originally the Stiff Kittens, they were later called Warsaw and made their first appearance at the Electric Circus, Manchester in May 1977.

Renamed Joy Division, they released an EP *An Ideal For Living* on their own label in June 1978. *Unknown Pleasures*, recorded at Strawberry Studios, was released on Tony Wilson's independent Factory Records in 1979 and powerful bass-driven tracks such as the menacing 'Shadowplay', 'Disorder', 'Day Of The Lords' and 'She's Lost Control' were critically acclaimed by the UK music press. Themes of crisis, darkness and failure permeated Curtis' lyrics and the album has been ranked as one of the 100 Greatest British Albums by Q magazine and one of the 'Fifty Coolest Records' by *Rolling Stone*.

In the wake of early success, Curtis found coping with 'live' performances increasingly difficult. Suffering from epilepsy and marital problems, he committed suicide a few days before Joy Division was due to embark on its first US tour in May 1980. The group's second album, *Closer* (1980), was released posthumously and 'Love Will Tear Us Apart' reached No. 13 in the UK singles chart. In the following year, Joy Division re-emerged as New Order with Sumner becoming lead vocalist. The band's story has been celebrated in two films: *24 Hour Party People* (2002) and *Control* (2007).

NEW ORDER

GILLIAN GILBERT
PETER HOOK
STEPHEN MORRIS
BERNARD SUMNER

New Order took over its post-Joy Division role, recruiting keyboard player Gillian Gilbert and performing regularly at sold-out live shows. They established themselves with Top 40 UK hit single 'Ceremony' and debut album *Movement* (1981), produced by Martin Hannett. The group toured the United States, Europe, Australia and New Zealand and in February 1983 they began recording with US dance producer Arthur Baker in New York.

In April 1983 their hypnotic 12-inch single 'Blue Monday' was a Top 20 hit. Its staccato dance riff powered up with menacing vocals would later return at No. 9 in the UK and worldwide sales would total over three million.

Power, Corruption And Lies reached No. 4 in the UK album chart in May. Their 12-inch single 'Confusion', produced and co-written by Arthur Baker, got to No. 12 in the UK. This was followed by 'Thieves Like Us', a melodic Top 20 UK hit in May 1984. New album *Low-Life* (1985) yielded the single 'The Perfect Kiss', a Top 5 US dance hit.

'True Faith', produced by Stephen Hague, was a world hit in 1987 and reached No. 4 in the UK, while its promo video was voted Best British Music Video at the 1988 Brit Awards. In 1989 their sixth album, *Technique*, shot straight to the top of the UK chart. New Order has continued to tour the world, acclaimed as one of the UK's most influential and successful New Wave electronic dance groups.

JOOLS HOLLAND OBE, DL

Having honed his left-hand boogie woogie skills in the days when every pub had a piano, Jools Holland went on to found the band Squeeze, form his own orchestra, become a star television presenter and transform New Year's Eve for millions of BBC TV viewers.

Born Julian Miles Holland in Blackheath, London (January 24, 1958), the singer, pianist and songwriter left Squeeze to go solo in 1978 but rejoined the reformed band in the late Eighties after co-hosting TV pop show *The Tube*. In 1987 he also formed his Big Band, which has grown into the current 19 piece Rhythm & Blues Orchestra, touring consistently for the past 20 years across the UK and the rest of Europe. Jools is also a successful recording artist; his long discography includes many illustrious collaborations, such as the multi-platinum selling series *Jools Holland And Friends*, with George Harrison, Bono, Chrissie Hynde and David Gilmour, and *The Golden Age Of Song* with Tom Jones, Amy Winehouse, Paul Weller and Jessie J among many.

Since 1982 Jools has promoted new talent and invited legendary musicians onto his BBC 2 TV show *Later...With Jools Holland* and his now traditional New Year's Eve *Hootenanny* as well as presenting an award-winning Radio 2 programme. He was awarded an OBE in 2003 for services to the British Music Industry and became Deputy Lieutenant for Kent in 2006. His best-selling autobiography *Barefaced Lies & Boogie Woogie Boasts* was published in 2007.

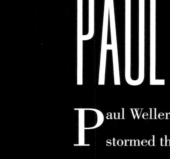

PAUL WELLER

Paul Weller, aka The Modfather, began his career with The Jam, who stormed the charts in 1979 with Weller's highly political hit 'The Eton Rifles'. Born in Sheerwater, Surrey (May 25, 1958), he led a band comprising old school friends and new blood. His father and manager got them their first bookings in local venues.

Although contemporaries of the London punk bands, The Jam best fitted the New Wave. After their first No. 1 with 'Going Underground', the band achieved many pop firsts including having two singles, unreleased in the UK, appear in the UK charts by dint of imports from Germany and Holland. Weller broke up The Jam in 1982 to form The Style Council. This band, leaning to more jazz, R&B and folk-based sounds, brought him his first hits in the US.

Weller went on to have a prolific solo career with the album *Stanley Road* putting him back in the charts.

He has released 11 solo albums and continues to top the charts, the last album *Sonik Kicks* also reaching No. 1 in 2012.

KATE BUSH CBE

A headset was fashioned from a coat hanger and radio mike to enable Kate Bush's early groundbreaking dance/song performances; this was one of the many 'firsts' attributed to the musician, singer/songwriter and record producer born in Welling, Kent (July 30, 1958).

She was the first woman to get a UK No. 1 hit with her own composition, 'Wuthering Heights' (1978), and the first British female artist to top the UK album charts (*Never For Ever*, 1980).

Her unique narrative style, some of which is inspired by wide-ranging literary and filmic influences, is infused with an eclectic use of instruments, including didgeridoo, uilleann pipes, balalaika and Fairlight. She set up her own publishing and management companies to ensure control of her work. Between 1978 and 2011 she released 10 albums. The most recent, critically acclaimed *50 Words For Snow*, features her son Bertie, along with Elton John and actor Stephen Fry.

She won a Brit Award as Best British Female Solo Artist in 1987 and received an Ivor Novello Award for Outstanding Contribution to British Music in 2002. She was appointed CBE in the 2013 New Year Honours for services to music.

IAN BROUDIE

Creator and artist behind the Lightning Seeds, Ian Zachary Broudie (born in Liverpool, August 4, 1958) was part of the post-punk scene in his home city in the late Seventies as a member of Big In Japan. Lightning Seeds' catchy pop songs include 'Three Lions', a football anthem that twice topped the UK charts.

The singer/songwriter, musician and record producer formed Original Mirrors (1979), then Care in the early Eighties. At the end of that decade his Lightning Seeds debut record 'Pure' hit the Top 20 and by the early Nineties he brought in other musicians to create a real band. The 1994 album *Jollification* confirmed the Seeds' position as a performing and touring outfit until 2000. Reforming in 2006, they continued with a new line-up, including Broudie's son Riley on guitar. The *Four Winds* album followed. His production skills have been utilised by many artists, notably Echo & the Bunnymen, The Zutons, The Coral, The Fall and Miles Kane. He released his debut solo album *Tales Told* in 2004.

DURAN DURAN

SIMON LE BON
NICK RHODES
JOHN TAYLOR
ROGER TAYLOR

Duran Duran brought glamour and energy to post-punk pop, fusing music, art, technology and fashion with a sense of style and confidence. First hitting the charts in the early Eighties, Simon Le Bon (vocals), Nick Rhodes (keyboards), John Taylor (bass), Andy Taylor (guitar), and Roger Taylor (drums) blended guitar rock, synth pop and melodic songs with strong lyrics. Their creation of new and exciting visuals helped transform music video and made them teen idols worldwide.

Duran Duran (named after a character in the sci-fi classic *Barbarella*) was formed in Birmingham in 1978 by school friends Nick Rhodes and John Taylor. After a few early line-up changes, drummer Roger Taylor joined the group followed by guitarist Andy Taylor and singer Simon Le Bon. In the months that followed, the band worked hard to gain a following, touring extensively before being signed to EMI.

Their debut album sold more than 2.5 million copies in the first year, staying on the charts for 118 weeks and producing the hit single 'Planet Earth', which reached No. 12 on the UK chart in March 1981. Further hits included 'Careless Memories' and 'Girls On Film'. In 1982, classic chart-toppers such as 'Hungry Like The Wolf', 'Rio' and 'Save A Prayer' turned Duran's second album, *Rio*, multi-platinum worldwide.

From 1983 the band dominated the charts, with 'Is There Something I Should Know' going straight to No. 1 in the UK and reaching No. 4 in the US. The third album, *Seven And The Ragged Tiger* (1984), made US No. 1, producing the single 'The Reflex'. In 1985 an invitation to write for the movie *A View To A Kill* secured another first when their song became the only Bond theme tune to make No. 1.

In 1985, the band underwent some line-up changes, with the departure of Andy Taylor and Roger Taylor. Warren Cuccurullo replaced Andy Taylor, forming a three piece that would last until 2002. Teaming up with Nile Rodgers, their first collaboration was the successful *Notorious* album.

In 1993, the band returned with multi-platinum *The Wedding Album* and US No. 1 single 'Ordinary World'. The song won them their first Ivor Novello Award. In 2004 the five original members reunited and released a new album *Astronaut*, from which '(Reach Up For The) Sunrise' was a UK Top 10 hit. Andy Taylor departed again in 2006. Since then, they have released two critically acclaimed albums, *Red Carpet Massacre* and *All You Need Is Now* – the latter making No. 1 in 15 countries on the iTunes charts. The band are currently working on their 14th studio release.

With more than 100 million records sold, Duran Duran have been the recipients of six Lifetime Achievement Awards (MTV, The Ivor Novellos, The Brits, The Spanish Ondas, GQ Magazine and Q Magazine). They have also been awarded several Grammys, two Ivor Novello Awards, a style icon award from the city of Milan and a star on the Hollywood Walk of Fame.

SADE

Helen Folasade Adu, credited as the most successful female artist in British history after selling more than 70 million albums, is known to her legions of fans worldwide as Sade. Born in Nigeria (January 16, 1959), Sade came to England aged four and settled in a small Essex village.

She studied fashion at St Martins School of Art, and through a series of coincidences ended up as a backing singer in the soul band Pride. Record companies grew interested in her and she reluctantly left Pride, signing with CBS to front the band Sade with three former Pride members (Stuart Matthewman, Andrew Hale and Paul Spencer Denman). Her unique style and distinctive voice took their first single 'Your Love Is King' to the top of the 1984 charts. A string of hits followed from their Brit and Grammy award-winning debut album *Diamond Life*.

In 2002 she made a rare British public appearance to accept an OBE, which she dedicated to all black women in England. Her most recent album, the first for ten years, was *Soldier Of Love* (2010), which reached No. 1 in 14 countries.

CRAIG ARMSTRONG OBE

Born in Glasgow (April 29, 1959), Craig Armstrong is an award-winning student of the Royal Academy of Music, graduating in 1981.

He is best known for his work in film, most notably his collaborations with director Baz Luhrmann. His score for *Romeo And Juliet* won him an Ivor Novello Award and a BAFTA Award, and in 2001 his *Moulin Rouge!* film score brought him BAFTA, Golden Globe and American Film Institute awards.

More recently, Armstrong wrote the music for Baz Luhrmann's film *The Great Gatsby* (2013). The soundtrack features his long-term collaborator, violinist Clio Gould, for whom he composed a violin concerto heard on his first classical album *Memory Takes My Hand* (2008).

In addition to writing award-winning scores for major Hollywood movies, Armstrong has written for the Royal Shakespeare Company, Royal Scottish National Orchestra and London Sinfonietta. He has worked with U2 and Madonna among other pop artists and his first opera was premiered in 2007 by Scottish Opera. He was appointed an OBE in 2010.

JAMES MacMILLAN CBE

Scottish composer and conductor James MacMillan's works reference Scottish traditional music as well as political and spiritual influences. A Roman Catholic, he composed the fanfare for the opening of the new Scottish Parliament in 1999.

Born in North Ayrshire (July 16, 1959), he studied composition at the universities of Edinburgh and Durham, where he gained a PhD in 1987. After two years lecturing in music at Manchester, he returned to Scotland. International acclaim attended the 1990 BBC Proms premiere by the BBC Scottish Symphony Orchestra of *The Confession Of Isobel Gowdie*, written while MacMillan was associate composer with the Scottish Chamber Orchestra. Among his many commissions was one from fellow Scot Evelyn Glennie for a percussion concerto, *Veni, Veni, Emmanuel* (1992). Mstislav Rostropovich premiered the cello concerto written for him in 1997. MacMillan's second opera *The Sacrifice* (2007) won a Royal Philharmonic Society Award and in 2008 he received the British Composer Award for Liturgical Music for his *Strathclyde Motets*. He was appointed a CBE in 2004.

GARY KEMP

Gary Kemp is one of the UK's most successful songwriters of the past 35 years. He is the guitarist and a founder member of Eighties super group Spandau Ballet. He was responsible for writing the words and music of all Spandau Ballet's 23 hit singles and albums, including modern-day standards such as 'Gold' and 'True' as well as classics such as 'Through The Barricades', 'Only When You Leave', 'To Cut A Long Story Short' and 'Chant No. 1'. His songs spent a combined total of over 500 weeks in the charts and were hits all over the world, generating over 25 million record sales and becoming part of the soundtrack to the Eighties.

Gary Kemp grew up in Islington (born October 16, 1959) and attended local grammar school Dame Alice Owens as well as Anna Scher's Children's Theatre drama club, becoming a child actor in film and TV before concentrating on playing guitar and songwriting.

Spandau Ballet split up in 1990 and Kemp decided to return to acting, starring in numerous films, including the hugely successful British crime thriller *The Krays* and Hollywood blockbuster *The Bodyguard*.

Kemp recorded an acclaimed solo album called *Little Bruises* and has written two musicals with Guy Pratt. One was *A Terrible Beauty* with Oscar-nominated book writer Shane Connaughton, about the relationship between the poet W. B. Yeats and the English aristocratic revolutionary Maud Gonne. The other, *The Bedbug*, had its debut at the National Theatre in 2004 and was co-written with Snoo Wilson. It was a re-imagined adaptation of Mayakovsky's 1922 play.

In 2009 Spandau reformed to successfully tour the world for the first time in 19 years. In the same year 4th Estate published Gary's memoir, *I Know This Much*. In 2012 Gary received an Ivor Novello Award for Outstanding Song Collection.

Photograph by Lucy Sewill, at Gary Kemp's home, November 11, 2013.

GEORGE BENJAMIN CBE

George Benjamin (born in London, January 31, 1960) was the youngest living composer ever to have music performed at the BBC Proms in 1980. His *Ringed By The Flat Horizon* had premiered earlier in the year at Cambridge while he was still a student of King's College. In the Seventies he was said to be Olivier Messiaen's favourite student at the Conservatoire de Paris, and since his assured debut, his reputation as a consummate craftsman has grown.

A conductor and pianist as well as composer, he taught at the Royal College of Music for 16 years before moving to King's College London (2001) where he succeeded Sir Harrison Birtwistle as Henry Purcell Professor.

His catalogue ranges from solo piano pieces (*Shadowlines*, 2001) to large orchestral works (*Sudden Time*, 1993). In recent years there have been festivals of his music in Aldeburgh, Frankfurt, Lucerne, Paris, London, Turin, Milan and San Francisco. His opera *Written On Skin* has been scheduled in over 20 venues around the world, including the Royal Opera House in London, since its premiere at the Aix-en-Provence Festival (2012). He was appointed a CBE in 2010.

Photograph by Lucy Sewill, The Royal Opera House, London, December 5, 2013.

U2

BONO (PAUL HEWSON KBE)
ADAM CLAYTON
THE EDGE (DAVID EVANS)
LARRY MULLEN, JR.

U2's '360°' concert tour from 2009 to 2011 was the highest attended and biggest grossing in history. It marked another milestone in the Irish band's worldwide success story that includes receiving a record 22 Grammy Awards and sales of 150 million records worldwide.

Singer Bono, lead guitarist The Edge, bass guitarist Adam Clayton and drummer Larry Mullen Jr came together as a post-punk school band in Dublin in 1976. They developed an eclectic style with rock and Irish folk influence. After early touring success in the Eighties, the group's album breakthrough came with *The Joshua Tree* in 1987. Throughout their career they have campaigned for human rights, their concern with social and political events expressed in their lyrics. In 1991 *Achtung Baby* was another major hit album. In 2005, U2's members were inducted into the Rock and Roll Hall of Fame.

MARK-ANTHONY TURNAGE

A composer of international stature, Mark-Anthony Turnage (born June 10, 1960) is indisputably among the most significant creative figures to have emerged in British music over the last three decades. His first opera, *Greek*, established Turnage's reputation as an artist who dared to forge his own path between modernism and tradition by means of a unique blend of jazz and classical styles.

Three Screaming Popes, *Kai*, *Momentum* and *Drowned Out* emerged during his time in residence with the City of Birmingham Symphony Orchestra with Simon Rattle, followed by *Blood On The Floor*, his unique score written for the distinguished jazz musicians John Scofield and Peter Erskine, and Martin Robertson.

His second full-length opera, *The Silver Tassie,* won both *The South Bank Show* and the Olivier Awards for Opera in 2001 and his third opera *Anna Nicole* played to sold-out houses at Covent Garden in 2011, and at its New York premiere performances in September 2013. Turnage has been resident composer with the Chicago Symphony Orchestra, BBC Symphony Orchestra and London Philharmonic Orchestra, and in 2013 began an association as featured composer with the London Symphony Orchestra. Recent works include new ballet scores for both Sadler's Wells and the Royal Ballet, a piano concerto and a percussion concerto.

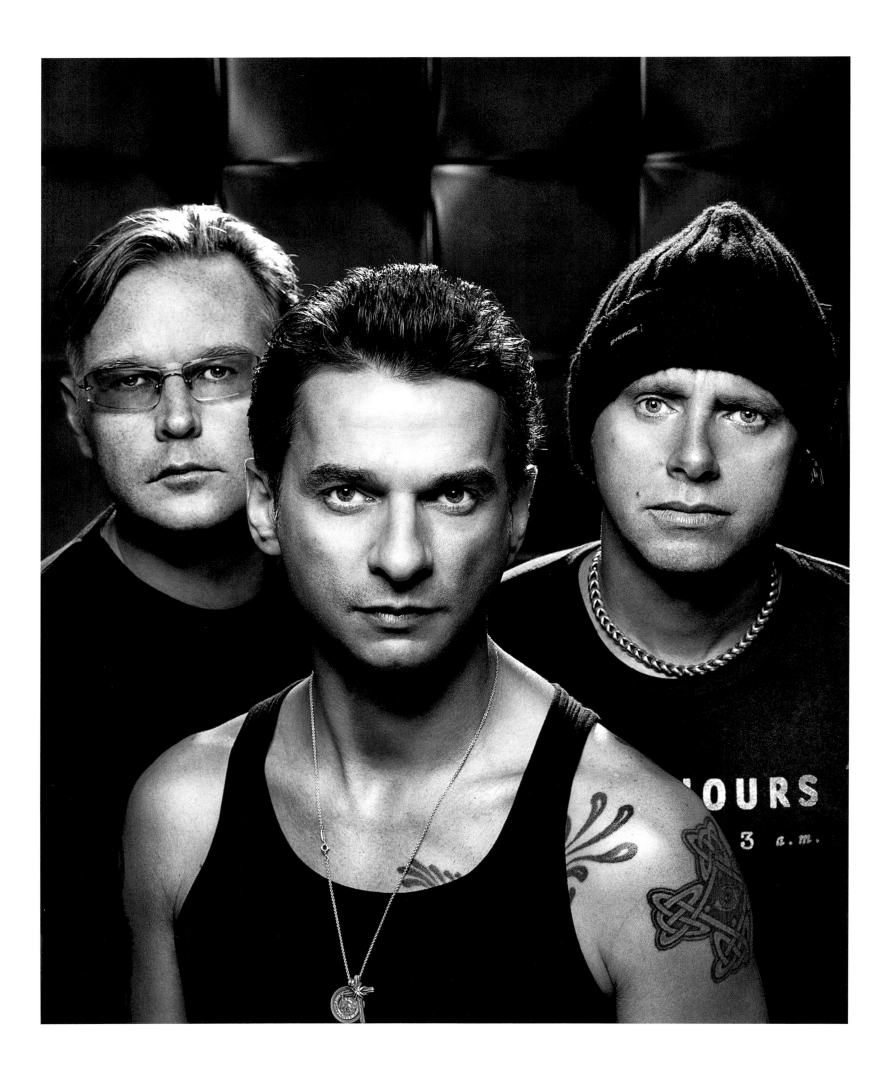

DEPECHE MODE

ANDY FLETCHER
DAVE GAHAN
MARTIN GORE

When 'People Are People' hit the US Top 20 in 1985, it marked a significant breakthrough for the innovative British group from Basildon. American chart success rewarded their struggle for recognition and bold dedication to creating new sounds. Hailed as pioneers of electronica, the keyboard/synthesiser-based group blended danceable themes with vocal harmonies, ultra-modern effects and an aura of mystery. The result has been a turbulent career lasting over 30 years as Depeche Mode have bequeathed a legacy of worldwide hit albums and singles.

The group formed in 1980 with Dave Gahan (lead vocals), Martin Gore (songwriter, keyboards, guitar and vocals), Andy Fletcher and Vince Clarke (keyboards). 'Depeche Mode' was suggested by design student Gahan, who spotted a French fashion magazine's use of the phrase meaning 'fast fashion'. Bookings at the Bridgehouse, Canning Town, and demo tapes led to the Mute label releasing 'Dreaming Of Me' (1981) followed by 'New Life', a UK No. 11 single.

Debut album *Speak & Spell* (1981) was a Top 10 hit, followed by *A Broken Frame* (1982), recorded after the departure of Vince Clarke, who went on to form Yazoo with Alison Moyet. He was replaced by Alan Wilder (keyboards, drums). Martin Gore, as the band's chief songwriter, embraced a wide range of lyrical topics from sex to religion, politics, loneliness and isolation.

After 'See You' got to No. 6 in the UK in January 1982, the group embarked on its first US tour. In 1984 wider international success saw 'People Are People' become both a US Top 20 hit and a No. 1 in Germany.

The Eighties albums *Some Great Reward*, *Black Celebration* and *Music For The Masses* consolidated their popularity, especially in America where they played to over 60,000 fans at the Pasadena Rose Bowl in 1988 and would go on to play sold-out US stadium shows. In 1990 Depeche Mode hit the US Billboard chart three times, with 'Personal Jesus' (28), 'Enjoy The Silence' (8) and 'Policy Of Truth' (15). 'Enjoy The Silence' won Best British Single at the 1991 Brit Awards.

Subsequent albums included the triple platinum *Violator*, the US and UK No. 1 *Songs Of Faith And Devotion* and *Ultra*, by which time the group had become a trio following Alan Wilder's 1995 departure.

In 2001 Depeche Mode released *Exciter* and toured 24 countries playing to over a million fans. In 2005 *Playing The Angel* was a No. 1 in 18 countries. Their twelfth studio album, *Sounds of the Universe*, was released in April 2009 followed by *Delta Machine* in March 2013.

Depeche Mode has had 50 songs in the UK Singles Chart and 13 Top 10 albums during their remarkable career. They have sold over 100 million albums and singles worldwide and been acclaimed as 'One of the greatest British pop groups of all time'.

DAVID ARNOLD

Born in Luton, Bedfordshire (January 23, 1962), David Arnold began writing film music for his friend Danny Cannon's student films after they had met as teenagers in a local arts centre.

Cannon eventually made his first feature, *The Young Americans*, in 1993 and asked Arnold to score it. Alongside the score, Arnold wrote the song 'Play Dead' with Bjork. It became a hit and the score was well received. This was soon followed by an offer for the film *Stargate*.

An unexpected hit, *Stargate* led to a relationship with its director Roland Emmerich and the pair went on to make *Independence Day* (for which David won a Grammy) and *Godzilla*. Other films include *Shaft, Zoolander, Narnia: Voyage Of The Dawn Treader, Hot Fuzz, Stepford Wives, Venus, Changing Lanes* and *2 Fast 2 Furious*.

In 1997, after producing an album of James Bond theme songs (*Shaken And Stirred*) covered by contemporary artists including Iggy Pop, Chrissie Hynde, Pulp and Leftfield, Barbara Broccoli and Michael G. Wilson asked David to score his first James Bond film, *Tomorrow Never Dies*.

John Barry recommended Arnold to Broccoli and the two became friends. David went on to score *The World Is Not Enough, Die Another Day, Casino Royale* and *Quantum Of Solace*.

Following Barry's death in 2011, Arnold helped to organise and performed at a star-studded memorial concert for his fellow Bond composer and friend at the Royal Albert Hall.

His television work includes music for *Little Britain* and *Sherlock* (with Michael Price) and he has collaborated with many groups and singers including Dame Shirley Bassey, Scott Walker, Kate Bush, The Who, Queen, Tinie Tempah, k. d. lang and Kaiser Chiefs.

David was musical director of the London 2012 Olympic and Paralympic Games closing ceremonies.

Photograph by Lucy Sewill, Air Studios, London, November 6, 2013.

JAZZIE B (TREVOR BERESFORD ROMEO, OBE)

The man who gave black British music 'a soul of its own' was born Trevor Beresford Romeo in Hornsey, London (January 6, 1963) but is better known as music producer and DJ Jazzie B. His BBC London radio show *Back 2 Life* showcases his musical arena from funk to reggae.

He was one of 10 children and began operating sound systems during the Sixties and Seventies. The name of the collective he founded, Soul II Soul (1988 – 1997), was originally also the name for his varied musical activities including sound systems. The list of artists for whom he has produced and remixed tracks runs from James Brown and Destiny's Child to Ziggy Marley and Sinéad O'Connor. A founding director of the Featured Artists Coalition, in 2002 he topped the business category list of 100 Great Black Britons and in 2008 was appointed OBE and received the first 'Inspiration' Ivor Novello Award for his pioneering work.

Photograph by Lucy Sewill, Soho Studios, London, February 3, 2014.

GUY CHAMBERS & ROBBIE WILLIAMS

When Robbie Williams left Take That in 1995, he launched a solo career like no other, becoming the UK's most successful solo artist and a global superstar. A charismatic, dynamic performer, the singer/songwriter (born in Stoke on Trent, February 13, 1974) enjoyed his first solo hit with 'Freedom' in 1996 and so began a tsunami of hit singles and albums from his debut *Life Thru A Lens* (1996) including the chart-topping anthem 'Angels'. *I've Been Expecting You* (1998), *Sing When You're Winning* (2000), *Swing When You're Winning* (2001, from which 'Somethin' Stupid' with Nicole Kidman became a major hit), and *Escapology* (2002) were all multiple gold and platinum albums and his *Greatest Hits* (2004) went six times platinum. *Rudebox* (2006) his seventh album to hit UK No. 1 was followed by *Reality Killed The Video Star* (2009) and *Take The Crown* (2012) featuring the UK No. 1 single 'Candy'. Robbie's record-breaking 17 Brit Awards include his Outstanding Contribution to British Music Award, presented in 2010. He has sold in excess of 57 million records.

A vital ingredient in Robbie's early success was the collaboration with record producer, songwriter and musician Guy Chambers (born in Hammersmith, London January 12, 1963). A student at London's Guildhall School of Music, Guy toured as a keyboard player with Julian Cope and with The Waterboys before joining World Party in 1986. In 1992 he formed The Lemon Trees and in 1997 was introduced to Williams. Guy co-wrote some of Robbie's best known hit singles including 'Rock DJ', 'Feel', 'Millennium', 'Let Me Entertain You' and 'Angels' with accolades including three Brit Awards, three Ivor Novello Awards and a Q magazine Classic Songwriter Award. Guy has written hits for artists including Kylie Minogue, Rufus Wainwright, Caro Emerald and Katy B and in 2012 he produced an all-star Christmas No. 1 charity single 'He Ain't Heavy…He's My Brother' for the families of victims of the 1989 Hillsborough football disaster.

The Williams/Chambers partnership has achieved six No. 1 UK albums and 17 Top 10 UK singles, including six chart toppers. They have recently collaborated again on *Swings Both Ways* (2013), their sixth album together. *Swings Both Ways* was the 1000th No. 1 to top the UK album charts.

GEORGE MICHAEL

Singer/songwriter and multi-instrumentalist George Michael exploded onto the British music scene as one half of Wham! Between 1981 and 1986 the duo dominated the charts with danceable hits such as 'Wake Me Up Before You Go-Go'.

Born Georgios Kyriacos Panayiotou (North London, June 25, 1963), Michael has garnered three Brit Awards, four Ivor Novello Awards, three American Music Awards and two Grammys.

He met Andrew Ridgeley at school in Hertfordshire and they later created Wham! Their first album *Fantastic* went to No. 1 in the UK and success in the United States followed. In 1985 Wham! were the first Western pop act to visit China. They split in 1986 and Michael's first solo single 'Careless Whisper' put him on the road to success.

He wrote, produced and played instruments on nearly every track of his 1987 album *Faith*, which spent 12 weeks at No. 1 in the US, spawned four US No. 1 hit singles and sold 25 million copies worldwide. *Faith* was followed by *Listen Without Prejudice Vol. 1* in 1990, another worldwide hit which included the single 'Freedom! '90'. A scene-stealing appearance at the Freddie Mercury Tribute concert in 1991 was followed by the *Five Live* EP and 'Jesus To A Child', a No. 1 single in the UK in 1994. The album *Older* (1996) featured 'Fastlove', another UK No. 1. Michael's place as one of the UK's best-loved artists was further cemented by the eight times platinum sales of *Ladies & Gentleman: The Best Of George Michael*, including new track 'Outside', another hit single.

Patience, his first album of new material in eight years, was released in 2003. A frenetic touring schedule over the following years took in the first gigs at the new Wembley Stadium, a guest appearance with Paul McCartney at Live 8 and two songs at the London 2012 Olympic Games closing ceremony.

In 2014 *Symphonica*, a record of his orchestral tour of the same name, went to No. 1, marking four decades of chart-topping albums.

COURTNEY PINE CBE

Courtney Pine's debut record *Journey To The Urge Within* (1986) was the first serious jazz album to make the British Top 40. The same year he formed the Jazz Warriors with young black jazz musicians, playing an exciting mix incorporating reggae, soul and Afrobeat. The band launched several solo careers and his promotion of jazz and inspirational projects for rising musicians continues.

Born in West London to Jamaican parents (March 18, 1964), Courtney studied clarinet at school, moving on to sax but also playing flute, bass clarinet and keyboards. He revived interest in jazz with his own albums, concerts and tours and by curating jazz festivals and nurturing young talent. His *Jazz Crusade* BBC Radio 2 programme ran for 12 series until 2008. Among several awards he was made CBE in 2009 for services to jazz music. His 14 albums include the latest *House of Legends* (2012).

NITIN SAWHNEY

Nitin Sawhney is a producer, composer and multi-instrumentalist whose diverse repertoire encompasses film scoring (over 50 films), solo album work (10 released to date), theatrical and dance work (including music for Cirque du Soleil, Complicite and regular collaborator Akram Khan) as well as extensive work for video games (primarily Ninja Theory) and many high-profile TV series (including the BBC's multiple BAFTA winning series *Human Planet*). Nitin has also produced for many acclaimed artists from Sir Paul McCartney and Sting to Joss Stone and Shakira, as well as producing his own radio series on BBC Radio 2 (*Nitin Sawhney Spins The Globe*).

Nitin has been the recipient of the 2000 Mercury Prize (for *Beyond Skin*), two Ivor Novello Award nominations, a MOBO Award, two BBC Radio 3 World Music Awards, a South Bank Show Award and five doctorates from different British universities. Nitin has also collaborated with and scored for the London Symphony Orchestra as well as many other leading orchestras across the world. As a DJ, Nitin has also released a number of successful club compilation albums, including *FabricLive.15*.

Photograph by Lucy Sewill, Studio One, January 21, 2014.

RADIOHEAD

JONNY GREENWOOD
COLIN GREENWOOD
ED O'BRIEN
PHIL SELWAY
THOM YORKE

Radiohead's debut 'Creep' (1992) appealed instantly to indie-rock fans, enticed by its despairing lyrics and angry guitars. The single was a worldwide hit for the innovative group, leading to the success of debut album *Pablo Honey*.

Thom Yorke (lead vocals, piano and guitar), Jonny Greenwood (lead guitar), Colin Greenwood (bass), Ed O'Brien (guitar) and Phil Selway (drums) formed On A Friday while at school in Abingdon, Oxford. Later at university the friends carried on rehearsing and playing local gigs before finding management and securing an EMI deal as Radiohead in 1991.

The band gained early support from radio DJs in Israel where their records were chart hits. US radio and MTV picked up on their music and 'Creep' was a Top 40 US hit. It also shot to No. 7 in the UK charts in 1993. Second album *The Bends* followed in 1995, yielding hit singles 'Street Spirit (Fade Out)' and 'High And Dry'. *OK Computer* (1997), the band's first UK No. 1 album, mixed melodic rock and avant-garde influences. Further releases *Kid A* (2000), *Amnesiac* (2001) and *Hail To The Thief* (2003) secured the group's artistic importance, while *In Rainbows* (2007) pioneered a new business model, offering listeners the choice to pay what they wanted to download the album.

NOEL GALLAGHER

Noel Thomas David Gallagher (born in Longsight, Manchester, May 29, 1967), hailed by George Martin as 'the finest songwriter of his generation', underpinned one of the most creative, successful and influential bands of the Nineties and beyond. Oasis heralded the Britpop era with their critically acclaimed debut album *Definitely Maybe* (1994) that yielded such powerful originals as 'Supersonic', 'Cigarettes & Alcohol', 'Rock'n' Roll Star' and the major hit single 'Live Forever'.

The group began life in 1991 as The Rain, formed by Noel's younger brother, vocalist Liam Gallagher. When Noel joined he became their lead guitarist and songwriter, noted for an outspoken personality and decisive approach to making music. The group now renamed Oasis was quickly signed by Alan McGee in 1994.

Definitely Maybe became the fastest-selling debut album in UK chart history and shot to No. 1. The second album, *(What's the Story) Morning Glory* (1995), produced by Noel and Owen Morris, featured string arrangements as well as the band's trademark biting guitar sound and intense vocals. Haunting and fiery songs like 'Champagne Supernova', 'Hello', 'Roll With It', 'Some Might Say', 'Wonderwall', 'Don't Look Back In Anger' and 'Morning Glory' led to Oasis becoming a worldwide rock phenomenon and one of the few British bands to enjoy major US success.

The album sold 347,000 copies in its first week on sale, was a UK No. 1 for 10 weeks and topped album charts worldwide. Intensive touring followed, including two landmark shows at Knebworth Park in August 1996 that drew a combined audience of 250,000.

(What's The Story) Morning Glory eventually sold 22 million copies worldwide and was voted 'Best UK Album' at the 1996 Brit Awards and 'Best UK Album of the Last 30 Years' at the 2010 Brit Awards.

Their third album, *Be Here Now*, became the fastest-selling album in UK chart history in 1997. *Standing On The Shoulders Of Giants* (2000) was followed by *Heathen Chemistry* (2002), *Don't Believe The Truth* (2005) and *Dig Out Your Soul* (2008), all of which went to No. 1 in the UK.

After the brothers parted company in 2009 following a breakdown in their relationship, Noel launched a solo career and formed Noel Gallagher's High Flying Birds the same year, their eponymous debut album going to No. 1 and selling 750,000 copies in the UK alone. Noel has also collaborated with fellow artists Paul Weller and the Chemical Brothers, with whom he had a No. 1 single with 'Setting Sun' (1996). He was declared 'Godlike Genius' at the 2012 NME Awards and received an Ivor Novello Award for Outstanding Song Collection in 2013.

DAMON ALBARN

F amed as frontman of Blur and co-founder of virtual group Gorillaz with Jamie Hewlett, Damon Albarn (born in Leytonstone, London, March 23, 1968) is a singer, songwriter, producer and composer whose eclectic musical style and observational lyrics have made him one of the UK's most influential and consistently interesting musicians.

Born out of a student band, Blur, comprising Albarn, Graham Coxon, Alex James and Dave Rowntree, released their first album *Leisure* in 1991. They went on to release another six albums including *Parklife*, one of Britpop's defining records that spent 90 weeks in the charts.

A change of mood, encompassing hip hop and dub, epitomised Gorillaz's eponymous debut record in 2001. The most successful virtual band ever followed up with *Demon Days*, *Plastic Beach* and *The Fall*, working with numerous guest artists and collaborators along the way including Lou Reed, De La Soul, Snoop Dog and Mos Def. In 2010 Albarn embarked on a Gorillaz world tour with a live band that included Mick Jones and Paul Simonon of The Clash and video animation, artwork and film by Jamie Hewlett.

Albarn's work outside Blur and Gorillaz includes *Mali Music* (2002), *The Good, The Bad & The Queen* (2006), *Kinshasa One Two* (2011) and *Rocket Juice & The Moon* (2012). His first full-length opera composition, *Monkey: Journey To The West*, premiered at Manchester International Festival in 2007, followed by *Dr Dee* (also at MIF) in 2011. Albarn has written music for film soundtracks *Ravenous* and *Broken* and most recently co-wrote and co-produced Bobby Womack's critically acclaimed album *The Bravest Man In The Universe*.

In October 2013, alongside Brian Eno and other international artists involved in the Africa Express collective, he travelled to Bamako to record the album *Africa Express Presents: Maison Des Jeunes* with local Malian musicians in just one week.

Albarn released his first solo album *Everyday Robots* in April 2014.

CATHY DENNIS

Cathy Dennis broke into the male-dominated world of hit songwriting in the early Nineties to become a five-times Ivor Novello Award and two-times Grammy Award winner by penning eight UK No. 1 singles, eight US Top 10 singles and global hits for a string of recording artists including Kelly Clarkson, Kelis, Pink and Christina Aguilera. Born in Norwich (March 25, 1969), she was spotted while recording demos at the age of 15 and was subsequently signed to Polydor Records. Her first success was as vocalist with DMob whose classic dance disc 'C'mon And Get My Love' peaked at No. 15 in the UK and hit the US Top 10. Three US solo hits followed and UK No. 1 singles for S Club Seven, but Dennis really hit her stride with the global phenomenon 'Can't Get You Out Of My Head' written with Rob Davis for Kylie Minogue in 2001. This was followed by Grammy winner 'Toxic' for Britney Spears, Sugababes' worldwide hit 'About You Now' and 'I Kissed A Girl' for Katy Perry, one of the biggest international selling pop songs ever. On top of everything else, Dennis also wrote the theme to *American Idol*.

Photograph by Lucy Sewill, at Cathy Dennis' home, January 20, 2014.

PJ HARVEY MBE

From the outset, PJ Harvey has commanded attention. She formed the eponymous bass/drums/guitar trio in 1991 in Dorset, England and by autumn had released the debut single 'Dress', which set the stage for a highly anticipated album release the following month. *Dry* was hailed as an astonishing debut, not just in the UK but also worldwide and especially in the US, where *Rolling Stone* magazine named Harvey Best Songwriter and Best New Female Singer.

Stories From The City, Stories From The Sea, Harvey's fifth studio album, was released in October 2000, winning the Mercury Music Prize in 2001.

In 2011, *Let England Shake* won Harvey her second Mercury Music Prize, entering her into the *Guinness Book Of Records* as the only artist to have achieved this.

A multi-instrumentalist, she is primarily a vocalist and guitarist while also an accomplished player of the autoharp. In addition to her musical career, PJ Harvey paints, draws, sculpts and writes poetry.

In December 2013, Harvey gave her debut public poetry reading at the British Library, and was a guest editor on BBC 4's *Today* programme. She was also awarded an MBE for services to music.

GARY BARLOW OBE

Gary Barlow has achieved fame as frontman and vocalist with the group Take That, as a songwriter and solo performer and as a judge on ITV's *The X Factor*. He has raised millions of pounds with charity concerts and projects and sold at least 50 million records worldwide.

Born in Cheshire (January 20, 1971), at age 15 he won a BBC TV songwriting contest and by the late Eighties was singing professionally. An introduction to casting agent Nigel Martin-Smith who was starting a 'boy band' led to Take That's rocket to fame with Barlow's songs. He has written for many other singers and 13 of his songs have topped the UK singles chart.

The Queen commissioned him to organise and produce her 2012 Diamond Jubilee celebrations and he was honoured with an OBE for his services to music and charity and given a prestigious Music Industry Trusts Award. Other accolades include six Ivor Novello Awards. Gary released a new solo album *Since I Saw You Last* in 2013.

THOMAS ADÈS

Thomas Adès (born in London, March 1, 1971) is a classical pianist and composer who dazzles critics and audiences with his inventive soundscapes. His orchestral works include *Asyla*, commissioned by the City of Birmingham Symphony orchestra, and his much-performed opera *The Tempest*.

Adès, a star student at the Guildhall School of Music and King's College, Cambridge, published his first opus *Five Eliot Landscapes* in 1990 and gave his first public piano recital aged 22. As composer, conductor and performer with many of the world's leading opera companies, he was voted Composer of the Year in the 2010 Classical Brit Awards. A retrospective of his work at the Barbican in 2007 included the premiere of *Tevot*, a work for Simon Rattle and the Berlin Philharmonic.

STEVE MAC & WAYNE HECTOR

Modern pop music has benefited greatly from the combined and individual talents of Steve Mac and Wayne Hector, two of the UK's most prolific and successful songwriters. The creative expertise of Mac/Hector has delivered a constant flow of hit records and global chart success for boy bands, contemporary dance acts, balladeers and mainstream pop stars on both sides of the Atlantic.

Steve Mac (born in Surrey, January 15, 1972) was taught piano from the age of eight but his interest in music as a career began when he was apprenticed with producer Nigel Wright in 1990. Mac has enjoyed an incredible track record of hits since 1991, with his first production 'Hear The Drummer Get Wicked' by Chad Jackson hitting No. 3 in the UK and his first co-written hit '(I Wanna Give You) Devotion' by Nomad peaking at No. 2 in the same year. Steve has since become one of Britain's most successful writer/producers, credited with 24 No. 1 singles in the UK and associated with over 150 hit singles and albums around the world.

In 2013 Mac received ASCAP's Songwriter of the Year Award along with Song of the Year for 'Glad You Came'. In 2012 he received the ASCAP Song of the Year Award for 'You Make Me Feel' by Cobra Starship. He has also won three BMI Awards, the MMF Producer of the Year, a MOBO Award and Brit Award in 2010 for JLS's 'Beat Again'. From his Rokstone Studios base in London's Parsons Green, he has provided hit records for a diverse range of artists including The Wanted, Westlife, Cobra Starship, One Direction, Shakira, Il Divo, John Newman, Susan Boyle, James Blunt, Kelly Clarkson, Ruben Studdard, Kate Winslet, Leona Lewis and many, many more.

Wayne Hector (born 1971) was initially groomed for stardom in his own right as a member of new jack swing act Rhythm N Bass, but a passion for the art of song diverted Wayne's talents in the direction of writing. Soon after Wayne first met Steve Mac the pair formed a creative partnership that quickly flourished: after delivering Damage's first Top 10 hit 'Forever', the duo masterminded hit after hit for Westlife. Over 30 smashes by the Irish band – including 'World Of Our Own' and 'Flying Without Wings' – have carried the Mac/Hector hallmark.

One of the most successful writers in the history of British pop, Hector has received numerous plaudits for his work. His accolades include a MOBO Award and two Brit Awards, one for JLS's 2010 No. 1 'Beat Again' and another for One Direction's 'Best Song Ever', which debuted at No. 1 in 65 countries. Wayne has been rewarded with multiple BMI and ASCAP Awards including honours for The Wanted's 'Glad You Came', Pussycat Dolls' 'I Hate This Part', Rascal Flatts' 'Feels Like Today', and Nicki Minaj's 'Starships', which won the R&B/Hip Hop Award for Song of the Year after selling a staggering 9 million units across the globe.

Hector's astonishing run of hits includes over 30 international No. 1s for a diverse array of artists including Nicki Minaj, Britney Spears, Tiesto, The Fray, Pussycat Dolls, The Wanted, Olly Murs, Christina Aguilera, Kylie Minogue, Mika, Labrinth, Kate Winslet, Def Leppard, Lionel Ritchie, Susan Boyle and Il Divo.

Photograph by Lucy Sewill, in the studio, January 28, 2014.

LIAM HOWLETT

Liam Howlett (born in Braintree, Essex, August 21, 1971) is a composer, producer and leader of electronic band The Prodigy, known for their angry, controversial lyrics and sound. The Prodigy was born in 1990 when Howlett was spotted by future members of the band playing his mixes from a van on beaches after raves. Performing an offshoot of acid house and as pioneers of the big beat genre, The Prodigy have sold more than 25 million records worldwide. Their first single 'Charly', containing a public information sample, was popular with the underground rave culture and reached No. 3 in the UK charts. Global success followed after their 1996 single 'Firestarter' topped the UK chart and gained US attention. Their third album *The Fat Of The Land* went in at No. 1 in 23 countries, including the US after its release coincided with the band headlining the opening night of the Glastonbury Festival in 1997. Their next two albums also went to No. 1 in the UK charts.

COLDPLAY

GUY BERRYMAN
JONNY BUCKLAND
WILL CHAMPION
CHRIS MARTIN

Poignant, affecting and melodic songs such as 'Spies', 'Don't Panic' and 'Yellow' introduced Coldplay to the world when *Parachutes* gently descended in the year 2000. Their acclaimed debut album marked the start of the new millennium and a hugely successful career for the group that features vocalist Chris Martin with Jonny Buckland (guitar), Guy Berryman (bass) and Will Champion (drums). They met as students at University College, London.

Chris and Jonny formed Starfish in 1996, subsequently renamed Coldplay in 1998. 'Yellow' was a major hit single and *Parachutes* was nominated for a Mercury Prize. It was followed by *A Rush Of Blood To The Head* (2002), *X&Y* (2005), *Viva La Vida (Or Death And All His Friends)* (2008) and *Mylo Xyloto* (2011), the latter topping album charts around the world.

Coldplay have won eight Brit Awards, seven Grammys and sold more than 60 million records worldwide. Martin also composes for solo artists and collaborated with rappers Jay-Z (on his 2006 album *Kingdom Come*) and Kanye West (*Graduation*, 2007). He is also an active campaigner for projects including Oxfam's Fair Trade operation.

MUSE

MATTHEW BELLAMY
DOMINIC HOWARD
CHRIS WOLSTENHOLME

When 'Time Is Running Out' hit the UK charts in 2003, the measured build-up of tension permeating the song exemplified the burning fuse that is the story of Muse. Their first Top 10 hit rewarded an exciting British band that brought together strands of classic rock musicianship with the highest standards of creative writing and performance.

Now one of the world's most successful groups, they experienced an early struggle for acceptance within the record industry. A string of hit albums and music business awards have since repaid their faith in their ambitious project.

The group from Teignmouth, Devon came together in 1994 with Matthew Bellamy (lead vocals, guitar, piano and keyboards, born June 9, 1978), Chris Wolstenholme (bass, vocals, keyboards, born December 2, 1978) and Dominic Howard (drums, percussion and synths, born December 7, 1977). While called Rocket Baby Dolls, the group won a local band contest, encouraging them to quit day jobs and change the band's name to Muse.

Producer Dennis Smith recorded their *Muse EP* (1998) at his Sawmills Studios in Cornwall, followed by the *Muscle Museum EP* (1999). UK record companies lacked interest in the band and they signed to US label Maverick. Debut album *Showbiz* (1999) featured poignant lyrics about relationships and the band's early struggles in their hometown. On *Origin Of Symmetry* (2001) they featured a powerful version of the Newley/Bricusse song 'Feeling Good'.

The band's interest in science fiction, literature and politics inspired many compositions and Matt Bellamy's intense vocal style was matched by the band's orchestral rock sound. They enjoyed Top 20 hits with the thunderous 'Hysteria', 'Sing For Absolution' and 'Butterflies & Hurricanes' amidst a stream of chart-topping albums: *Absolution* (2003), *Black Holes And Revelations* (2006), *The Resistance* (2009, showcasing the classically influenced 'Exogenesis Symphony') and *The 2nd Law* (2012).

As fan support proliferated, Muse embarked on major tours of the UK, North America, Australia, New Zealand and Europe. Landmark events included their performances at Glastonbury Festival (2004 and 2010), Madison Square Garden, New York (2007) and the SXSW Festival Austin, Texas (2010).

Muse have sold more than 15 million albums throughout the world and received multiple awards, including the O_2 Silver Clef presented by Queen's Roger Taylor and Brian May. They have also won press awards for Best Live Act, Best Album and Best British band and in 2011 a Grammy for Best Rock Album for *The Resistance*. They have also received an Ivor Novello Award for International Achievement.

AMY WINEHOUSE

Amy Jade Winehouse (born in Southgate, London, September 14, 1983), whose emotional low tones echoed the great American jazz divas, scored major successes during her short career. Her second album *Back To Black* (2006) made her the first British female to win five Grammy Awards, including Best New Artist and Song of the Year.

She also won three Ivor Novello Awards, including Best Contemporary Song for 'Rehab', which referenced her struggles with alcohol and drugs. Growing up in a family with strong jazz ties (her grandmother was a singer and several uncles were jazz musicians), she was encouraged to attend theatre school, making an early TV appearance with other pupils on *The Fast Show*.

A songwriter since her teens, she was vocalist with the National Youth Jazz Orchestra (2000) before a friend sent her demo tape to an A&R person and excited music industry managers vied for her attention. *Frank*, the title of her first album, was an acknowledgement of Sinatra's influence.

Her other awards included the 2007 Brit Award for Best British Female artist. After her death on July 23, 2011 from alcohol poisoning, *Back To Black* posthumously became the best-selling UK album of the new millennium.

DIZZEE RASCAL

The songwriter and record producer born Dylan Kwabena Mills (born October 1, 1985) is known as Dizzee Rascal by fans of hip hop, R&B, UK garage, bassline and grime music. Raised by his Ghanaian mother in London's East End after his Nigerian father died, Dizzee had a troubled school career until he began composing music on a school computer. As a pirate radio DJ he started winning fans with experimental use of decks and styles. He produced his first single 'I Luv U' in 2002, the same year he formed the Roll Deep Crew, a garage collective, with former school friends.

Best-known hits are the No. 1 'Dance Wiv Me', 'Holiday', 'Dirtee Disco' and 'Shout'. His debut album *Boy In Da Corner* won the 2003 Mercury Prize. Critical approval greeted subsequent albums, *Showtime* and *Maths+ English* followed by *Tongue N' Cheek* which went platinum. His 2013 album *The Fifth* features Robbie Williams on the lead single 'Goin' Crazy'. He has formed his own record label Dirtee Stank and is a patron of the summer music workshops run by Futureversity in Tower Hamlets, which he attended as a teenager.

Photograph by Lucy Sewill, Dirtee Stank Studio, London December 11, 2013.

ADELE (ADELE ADKINS, MBE)

A stunning voice and heart-rending lyrics catapulted Adele to critical and popular acclaim soon after a friend posted her demo on Myspace. Adele Laurie Blue Adkins, MBE, singer/songwriter and multi-instrumentalist, was 'the voice' of 2008, the year she won the first Critics' Choice Brit Award.

Born in Tottenham, London (May 5, 1988), her singing began aged four as she imitated the Spice Girls. At 16 she wrote her first recorded song 'Hometown Glory' and as a South London teenager she immersed herself in the sounds of Etta James and Ella Fitzgerald, but other influences include Beyoncé and Gabrielle.

A graduate of the Brit School for Performing Arts, Adele's debut album *19* charted both sides of the Atlantic and won her first two Grammy Awards. Her second album, *21*, including 'Someone Like You' and 'Rolling In The Deep', made her the first artist since The Beatles to have two Top 5 hits in both singles and album charts. She went on to win in six categories at the 2012 Grammy Awards. Adele also won an Oscar for writing the Bond theme 'Skyfall'.

ED SHEERAN

Ed Sheeran created a sensation with his 2011 debut album entitled + that yielded the hit singles 'The A Team' and 'Lego House'. Blessed with an emotive, melodic vocal style and delicate acoustic guitar technique, his lyrics are touching and perceptive. Elton John is among supporters who gave the singer/songwriter early encouragement. Born in Halifax, West Yorkshire (February 17, 1991), Sheeran grew up in Framlingham, Suffolk where he sang in a church choir and learned to play guitar. Writing songs at school, he moved to London in 2008 to pursue his career in music. Visiting Los Angeles in 2010 he sang at open mic nights and was spotted by Jamie Foxx's manager, which led to appearances on the actor's radio show and access to his recording studio. In 2011 Sheeran released the independent EP *No. 5 Collaborations Project* that led to a contract with Asylum. After an appearance on BBC TV's *Later...With Jools Holland*, 'The A Team' became a best-selling single of the year. In February 2012 Sheeran received Brit Awards for Best British Male Solo artist and British Breakthrough of the Year.

THE SOCIETY OF DISTINGUISHED SONGWRITERS

Silence may be golden but difficult to achieve whenever meetings of the Society of Distinguished Songwriters are held. It is, after all, a convivial gathering of exuberant souls for whom making music has been a lifetime's work – and pleasure. That their work has also brought pleasure to millions around the world is another cause for celebration.

The SODS, as they are invariably known, form an exclusive brethren responsible for creating some of the greatest hit songs of the last 50 years. The simple yet brilliant idea to bring them together occurred to the society's founder, Mitch Murray, in 1971: 'We all got on so well as songwriters and all the guys like Tony Hatch and Les Reed knew each other and socialised. So I thought it would be nice to have our own private supper club – with a difference.'

The SODS' aim was to: 'Have a lovely time and enjoy each other's company.'

Murray met with approval at the society's initial meeting, when basic ground rules were agreed. Black tie and evening dress must be worn at 'over the top' banquets. However, exceptions are made for free spirits who prefer a T-shirt and bandana or in the case of Scottish composers, a sporran and kilt.

'There's nothing very democratic about the SODS. You only need 75% of members at any meeting voting 'yes' for somebody to be elected. When we started everyone was roughly the same age. Nowadays we have people in their twenties and eighties as the generation gap has grown wider.'

Most meetings take place in a hotel or restaurant and a new 'King Sod' is elected every year. His role is to run the society, selecting menus and venues. Mitch Murray was the first king and he was re-elected in 1992 as King Sod XXI. Past kings include Roger Cook, Gary Osborne and Mike Batt. Justin Hayward, composer of 'Nights In White Satin', was His Majesty in 2013. The kings don't insist on regal formality when they have an audience at court.

Murray: 'We don't talk business but tell jokes, have singsongs standing around a piano and laugh a lot. Les Reed or Tony Hatch plays the piano and Bruce Welch and Marty Wilde bring their guitars. You never hear our own songs being played funnily enough. We usually end up playing Beach Boys hits!'

The SODS have three meetings a year and a special Ladies' Night when guests including wives and girlfriends are invited. At the 2013 Ladies' Night, held in December at London's Savoy Hotel, the guests included Cilla Black, Jimmy Tarbuck and many other stars. It was a night to remember when some of the members relented and sang their own songs with Les Reed performing 'Delilah', Tony Hatch singing 'Downtown' and Don Black singing 'Born Free' to a standing ovation.

Whenever SODS gather, expect noise, fun and a lot of remarkable music. Long may they reign.

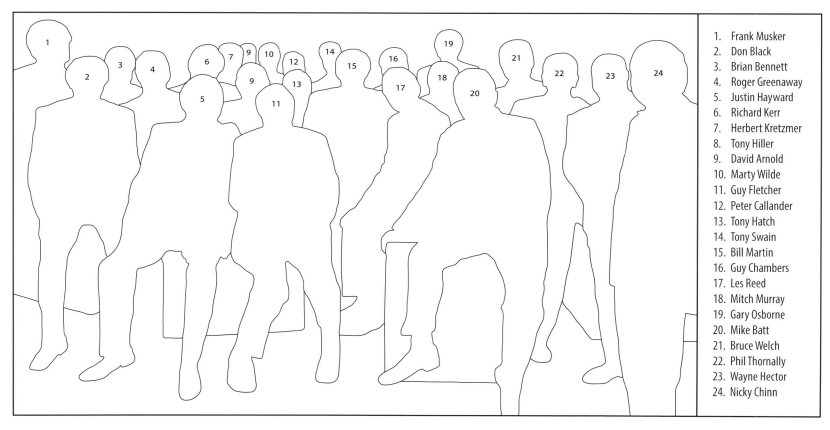

1. Frank Musker
2. Don Black
3. Brian Bennett
4. Roger Greenaway
5. Justin Hayward
6. Richard Kerr
7. Herbert Kretzmer
8. Tony Hiller
9. David Arnold
10. Marty Wilde
11. Guy Fletcher
12. Peter Callander
13. Tony Hatch
14. Tony Swain
15. Bill Martin
16. Guy Chambers
17. Les Reed
18. Mitch Murray
19. Gary Osborne
20. Mike Batt
21. Bruce Welch
22. Phil Thornally
23. Wayne Hector
24. Nicky Chinn

PHOTO CREDITS

Archive photo research by Jacqui Black

CHRIS WELCH

Chris Welch, former features editor of *Melody Maker*, is the author of more than 30 books on rock and pop music. He joined the *Kentish Times* in 1962 and reported on local beat groups Sounds Incorporated and the Rolling Stones.

In October 1964 Chris joined *Melody Maker* as a staff writer and interviewed a host of stars and groups including Burt Bacharach, Diana Ross, Paul McCartney, Marc Bolan, Jimi Hendrix, David Bowie, Elton John and Led Zeppelin.

In the 1970s Chris wrote extensively about Prog Rock groups Pink Floyd, Deep Purple, Genesis, Yes and ELP. In 1979 he became assistant editor of *Musicians Only*, covering the rise of The Buggles and Adam Ant. During the 1980s he was reviews editor for *Kerrang!* and editor of *Metal Hammer*.

His books include *Hendrix: The Biography* and *Ginger Geezer: The Life Of Vivian Stanshall*. His latest books are *David Bowie: A Life In Pictures* and *Eric Clapton: Treasures* (both Carlton, 2013).

In 2012 Chris was awarded a BASCA Gold Badge Of Merit for his special contribution to the British music industry.

LUCY SEWILL

Lucy Sewill is a photographer best known for her perceptive portraits of major British celebrities. She specialises in one-on-one informal personal portraiture. Lucy's work has been published worldwide, with commissions from major publishing houses and magazines. Her work has appeared in national newspapers.

She specialises in the worlds of music, broadcasting, politics, theatre and opera. She works closely with a number of leading journalists and writers.

Her work has been exhibited at the National Portrait Gallery and a number of her portraits are held in the collection.

Amongst the many well-known faces she has captured are David Cameron MP, Boris Johnson, Dame Edna Everage, Terry Wogan, Tony Benn, Kate Adie, Phil Collins, Hugh Fearnley-Whittingstall and Justin Fletcher.